To Ray McConnell

with Best Wishes

Hal Fredericks

August, 1991

BRICKLIN

BRICKLIN

by

H. A. Fredericks

with

Allan Chambers

Brunswick Press
Fredericton, N.B.

(Perfect Bound)
ISBN 0 88790 087 9

(Hard Case)
ISBN 0 88790 088 7

Printed and bound in Canada By Unipress Ltd., Fredericton, N.B.

To those who gave generously
of their thoughts,
their experiences,
and their files —
with candor.

And to my sons.

— H. A. F.

Table of Contents

Chapter 1

THE MOST BEAUTIFUL CAR

The twin-engine plane carrying Premier Richard Bennett Hatfield of New Brunswick, several reporters and a large crate of fresh Atlantic salmon landed in New Jersey late on the afternoon of June 24, 1974. A man in chauffeur's gear met the plane. He gave the salmon a sour look and led the group to a limousine for the trip into New York City. The reporters were deposited at a downtown hotel and the limousine drifted back into the traffic, with Hatfield inside. He had a busy two days ahead: meetings, a television appearance, a salmon dinner. The next day he would attend an unveiling of the Bricklin car, in which his government had an investment.

Hatfield had waited a long time for the New York ceremony. Malcolm Bricklin, the car's Philadelphia-born promoter, had promised earlier that production would begin at New Brunswick plants in September, 1973. Bricklin had collected franchise fees and deposits from car dealers in the U.S., and now the dealers were becoming anxious. In April, 1974, Hatfield's government had provided new financing for Bricklin, and people in New Brunswick were asking questions. Where were the cars?

The Four Seasons hotel at Park Avenue and Fifty-Second Street, where Bricklin had rented a ballroom for $50,000, was crowded on Tuesday, June 25. The guest list, compiled with the help of Rogers and Cowan, Inc., a public relations firm with offices in Beverly Hills and on Madison Avenue, included government and bank officials, media representatives, Bricklin dealers and car hobbyists, and a collection of Park Avenue people in well-cut suits and plunging necklines. After the preliminary speeches, Malcolm Bricklin jumped onto a platform and pulled a sheet from a pearl-white fastback. The crowd, guarding cocktails, jostled for a look. Albert Bricklin, Malcolm's father, strode onto the platform with a hot branding iron in his hand. "I name this car 'Bricklin,' " Albert said, pressing the iron to the car's body. There was smoke. Malcolm assured the crowd that, because of the car's unique acrylic body, the brand (a stylized B) could be simply buffed away. The crowd was impressed.

Throughout the afternoon, people inspected prototype models of Bricklin's car. They played with the gull-wing doors (which opened upwards, not sideways) and tested their knuckles on the gleaming acrylic. Sammy Cahn, a veteran Broadway composer who was hired by

Rogers and Cowan to sing a song, climbed onto a stage and sang. "The most beautiful car in the world," Cahn crooned, "Counting tall cars, counting small cars."

Hatfield and Bricklin basked in the attention.

"I've invested a lot of faith in this car," confessed Hatfield, whose government's investment in the car stood at nearly $5 million, "and I'm very, very happy."

So was Bricklin. Dressed in a white, bell-bottomed leisure suit and print shirt (even Cahn, the songwriter, felt compelled to ask what the clothes cost), Bricklin bobbed in and out of the crowd, accepting handshakes and offering comments. He would be building 1,000 cars a month by October, he predicted. His car, he said, had every safety device the U.S. government would require in the next few years, "and some they won't even think of." Soon, he said, the Big Three automakers would be rushing to imitate the Bricklin.

Equally assertive were the press kits prepared by Rogers and Cowan and distributed to the crowd by two of Bricklin's sons, Craig and Kevin. (Rogers and Cowan would play a large role in promoting the Bricklin car in the next year. The firm had already managed to put Hatfield and Albert Bricklin, complete with branding iron, on the highly-rated *Today Show*. In coming months, Jonas Halperin, an official with Rogers and Cowan, would use his skills to put the Bricklin car on the pages of most leading U.S. car magazines. Halperin also made arrangements for a special *Playboy* feature on the Bricklin — the issue containing the feature sold out in New Brunswick in two days, and has since become a local collector's item). The Rogers and Cowan kits were distributed in suede briefcases that matched the upholstery in the Bricklin car. "Will introduction of the Bricklin safety car to the U.S. automobile market spark an international revolution in automaking?" asked one of the press releases in the kits. "Malcolm Bricklin, 35-year-old president of Phoenix-based General Vehicle Inc., America's newest automobile manufacturer, is convinced that his car's vacuum-formed acrylic body will be widely emulated in the near future." Another release devoted itself to Bricklin's "remarkable business acumen," and yet another described his production plans — "12,000 cars in the first year of operation, and 100,000 cars at the end of four years."

Truth, now. People who were accustomed to hearing Bricklin talk in terms of thousands of cars could not have guessed the amount of effort and waste that went into the production of three prototype cars for the New York show. The cars' bodies were made by hand. In June, 1974, nine months after Bricklin said he would be in production, company technicians in New Brunswick were still experimenting with processes for bonding fibreglass and acrylic, the two body components in Bricklin's revolutionary car. Bricklin, for all his remarkable business acumen, had assumed mistakenly that the plastics industry had the technology to do it. Officials of the New Brunswick government, who provided financing to Bricklin in 1973 on the strength of some dubious projections and a short car film that Bricklin carried with him, had not known enough to ask any questions. Car bodies for the New York show were formed manually, an arduous process that involves the hand-shaping of body moulds for the acrylic, and the hand-laying of fibreglass in the acrylic. (A bizarre note: When officials of the New Brunswick Research and Productivity Council were requested in May, 1974, a month before the New York show, to join the search for a bonding formula, they asked if Bricklin officials had developed tests to determine if the two body components were truly stuck. The response: Albert Bricklin proposed to strike each part with a seven-pound hammer. If the part didn't fly apart, it was stuck. With notions like this, Albert Bricklin managed to antagonize nearly every experienced production man who worked under him on the Bricklin car.)

At the time of the New York show, the New Brunswick government had provided financing of $4.5 million for Bricklin's car. The money had been advanced on the assumption that Bricklin needed initial financing to begin the production of cars. By the time the New Brunswick government discovered its error, it would have paid for the engineering and development of Bricklin's car. By that time, it would also be paying many of the costs, including salaries, of keeping Bricklin's U.S. complex of companies in operation. Fifteen months after the New York opening, the government's investment in Bricklin would be a dizzying $23 million, an amount equal to about $30 for each of the province's 670,000 citizens. Bricklin's car would plunge the province into controversy. An orange Bricklin would become an election symbol, Hatfield's promise of a better New Brunswick. In September, 1975, Bricklin's car company would collapse, after building 2,880 cars.

According to Bricklin company sources, the cost of the first cars to roll off the assembly line at Saint John, New Brunswick in the fall of 1974 was more than $50,000 apiece. Vast amounts of acrylic and fibreglass were scrapped in the process of building a few car bodies. The problems of bonding and parts breakage, which had set back production a full year, were never adequately resolved. The scrap rate on body parts in the last months before Bricklin's collapse ranged from 15 to 25 per cent. Labor costs were enormous. According to Bricklin sources, the average cost of the first 800 cars built by Bricklin was $16,000 apiece. According to operating loss figures, which the New Brunswick government still considers to be confidential, the cost of the 2,880 cars built in Bricklin's only year of production was more than $13,000 apiece. A $6,500 selling price announced by Bricklin at his New York opening was nonsense. So was a $2,200 wholesale price stipulated in the initial 1973 financial agreement between Bricklin and New Brunswick. The wholesale price was increased eventually to $5,400. At that price, Bricklin Canada Ltd., the New Brunswick company that manufactured cars, lost at least $8,000 on every car it sold to Bricklin's U.S. sales organization, which in turn sold the cars to dealers, at a profit. The wholesale price was finally increased to $7,200 in 1975. At that price, the New Brunswick company lost at least $5,000 on each car. The Bricklin collapse was inevitable.

The New Brunswick government exercised virtually no accounting controls over the money it provided to Bricklin. Government officials took the position that they didn't know how to operate a car company. They didn't realize that they knew as much as Bricklin. For much of the production period, Bricklin's accounting records, including those of the New Brunswick company, were kept in New York. Loans were advanced by the government on the basis of fiscal projections prepared by Bricklin's accountants, who referred privately to the projections as "selling statements." Throughout much of the production period, the only budgetary and production goals requested by the government were of the sort that Bricklin would provide gladly to anyone within earshot. In these circumstances, Bricklin ran up production losses in New Brunswick of a staggering $16.6 million by June 30, 1975. At the same time, his complex of U.S. companies reported losses of $6 million. Even these figures are understated. They are unaudited figures provided to the government by Bricklin's accountants. They don't include, for example, the piles of bills that were simply thrown into boxes and files in the offices of Bricklin Canada Ltd. in the summer of 1975. The New Brunswick government had so little control over Bricklin's accounting practices that, after the collapse, it would not know how much money had been diverted from the New Brunswick company to Bricklin's U.S. operations.

In late 1974, with its investment beginning to mushroom, the New Brunswick government made efforts to control Bricklin's spending. Consultants and accountants were appointed. The efforts culminated with the appointment of Clarkson Gordon & Company in the summer of 1975 to prepare a detailed operating budget for Bricklin Canada Ltd. and Bricklin's U.S. companies. It would be the first detailed budget to be prepared for the Bricklin companies since they began operations.

The Clarkson Gordon Company reported on September 23, 1975, two years too late. Its report, which the government still considers to be confidential, said that Bricklin would continue to sustain losses in 1976, and would require further government loans. Bricklin had already requested another $10 million in August. Two days after the government received the Clarkson Gordon report, it put Bricklin Canada Ltd. in receivership.

Fifteen months after the New York opening, Bricklin's plants in New Brunswick would be locked. Hatfield's government would be facing a crisis of confidence. It was not an outcome that most of the people at the New York opening, including Hatfield and Bricklin, would have predicted. Granted, one of the cars at the ceremony lacked a radiator. Granted, the cars' doors were wired to a generator under the platform to ensure that they would open and close all day. Granted, the technician who drove one of the cars from Saint John to New York had not dared to travel over 35 miles an hour for fear he would lose the shock absorbers. Granted, there were production problems. Granted, Bricklin would soon have to ask New Brunswick for a lot more money. Granted all these things, Malcolm Bricklin was jubilant as he floated back and forth across the Four Seasons ballroom. So was Hatfield, who still bore the look of a man who had bounded onto the platform earlier in the day to plant a kiss on Diane Davies, a blonde model who had been hired to lounge for an afternoon on the hood of a white Bricklin — New Brunswick's car.

Chapter 2

THE ROAD TO NEW BRUNSWICK

Bricklin's background, which the New Brunswick government didn't investigate, wasn't that of a car manufacturer. His car was the end result of an erratic progress from business deal to business deal, in which a lot of enemies were made. By the time he was twenty-five, Bricklin's name was on half a dozen lawsuits. By the time he was thirty-five, it was on more lawsuits. By that time, he was knocking on New Brunswick's door. He had debts of $2 million and he had a short film of a car he wanted to build. He had a rented plant near Detroit and a handful of employees. The car in the film was a hand-fashioned prototype. It had never been engineered. New Brunswick's officials, including Hatfield, didn't appreciate the difference. They financed him. The New Brunswick officials would learn slowly that they had financed little more than a dream. By that time, the province's investment in Bricklin's car would have risen to $23 million. By that time, too, Bricklin's dreams would have taken on King Kong proportions. When his car company was collapsing in the late summer of 1975, Bricklin confessed a private dream to close friends. He wanted to buy the Empire State Building and use it as his world headquarters.

Bricklin's adventures in business before he arrived in New Brunswick had, for all their twists and turns, a pattern to them. Everything he touched turned to franchises. After he found New Brunswick, Bricklin sold car franchises even before he had an assembly line. Franchises are promotions. They are an idea sold for a fee. If the idea catches on (MacDonald's hamburger outlets, for example), the fees can be very lucrative. Bricklin discovered franchises early in his business life. By the time he reached New Brunswick, they were almost a reflex action with him: Think of an idea and franchise it. But his first franchises, which he sold in the early 1960s, got him into trouble. So would some of his later franchises.

In 1958, Bricklin dropped out of the University of Florida, where, he once quipped, he had majored in time and space. He was nineteen and married. He established a building supplies business in Orlando, Florida. His father, Albert, who had moved the Bricklin family to Florida from Philadelphia when Malcolm was ten, had operated a building supplies store in Orlando. Malcolm could draw on established lines of credit and suppliers. It was a secure life, but after a couple of years it wasn't enough. Bricklin was learning about business. "I was twenty-one, married, paying maybe $150-a-month rent on the house we were living in," he said in a 1975 interview. "I had a nice little sports car, not new but nice. I didn't owe a single penny and I was very proud of that, okay?

"So one day I walk into the bank where I had my savings account and just for the hell of it I say, 'I'd like to take out a small loan.' The loan manager says, 'We can't make you a loan, Mr. Bricklin, you don't have any credit.' 'What do you mean I don't have any credit,' I say. 'I don't owe anybody a cent. Besides which, I have more money in my savings account than I want to borrow.' 'Sorry, the only way you can get a loan is to establish credit.' 'You mean if I already owe somebody money I can get a loan, but if I don't owe anybody anything I can't?' 'That's right, Mr. Bricklin.'

"So I go home, get the title to my car, take it back to the bank and have them finance it. Then I take the finance papers to the loan manager of the same bank and say, 'Okay, I owe money, can I get a loan now?' 'Absolutely,' he says. I get the loan, go home and say, 'Brenda, open a charge account in every store in Orlando. From now on we don't pay cash for anything.' "

Bricklin began to dream of something more than a corner store in Orlando. Using his new credit rating, he expanded his little business to include three stores in the city. He developed the idea of a chain of hardware stores stretching beyond Orlando. His first move was the formation of a new company. In coming years, Bricklin's first move whenever he had a saleable idea, or occasionally an unsaleable one, would be the formation of a company or cluster of companies, usually with an abstract name like General, Universal or International. To launch his hardware chain, Bricklin formed Handyman America, Inc. He didn't possess the money to establish the chain himself, but he intended to persuade other people to invest in him. The idea, as Bricklin developed it, would be the sale of franchises in the Handyman name. Investors would have the chance to share in a revolutionary form of hardware merchandising. For a franchise fee of about $15,000, investors would have access to Handyman advertising and to stocks of merchandising from a centrally-located Handyman warehouse. Handyman would line up suppliers and would maintain an agreed-upon amount of merchandise in the franchise stores. Investors would return money from sales to Handyman and would receive a cheque based on sales, plus a replenishing of their stocks. Handyman store owners would keep their stores open from nine in the morning until nine in the evening, seven days a week. Long hours and controlled inventories, in addition to the recognizeable Handyman name, would return sizeable profits to the store operators. Essentially, Bricklin would do for hardware what Colonel Sanders did for fast food places. Bricklin thought the idea would sell. He quickly brought his family into the project, as he would in all his subsequent businesses. His father, Albert, was retained to sell franchises, at $1,000 per franchise. Malcolm's uncle, Ben Bricklin, loaned money to help finance Handyman. Malcolm's mother, Gertrude, was hired as a bookkeeper. Bricklin began to look for investors.

Bricklin quickly realized that the return on the sale of individual franchises wouldn't be enough to finance his central warehouses or the development of a widespread chain. He had to generate more money. He developed his franchise system to include the sale of Handyman licences for different regions. Buyers of the licences would have exclusive rights to develop Handyman franchises in a designated territory, such as the western states. An investor would pay $250,000 for a Handyman licence. Bricklin would later claim that he parlayed this system into a nation-wide chain of 147 Handyman stores, and that in 1964, anxious to find new challenges, he was able to sell his interest in Handyman for $1 million after taxes. He had always wanted to be a millionaire by the time he was twenty-five, he would say. Advertising distributed by Rogers and Cowan at the New York opening would describe Bricklin as a "self-made millionaire at age 25," who had developed "today's nation-wide Handyman franchise system." However, lawsuits launched by several people to whom Bricklin sold Handyman territorial licences in 1964, when his Handyman chain was at a peak of about 18 stores, tell an altogether different story. The lawsuits say that Handyman was a losing operation. They also claim that Bricklin defrauded several licence purchasers out of hundreds of thousands of dollars.

On November 30, 1964, three California businessmen launched actions in California Superior Court alleging that Handyman America, Inc., Malcolm Bricklin and Albert Bricklin defrauded them of money. Vernon E. Fish, Harold S. Hassel and James R. Bair claimed that on the basis of false figures provided to them by Malcolm Bricklin, they made a down payment of $95,000 to Handyman America, Inc. for a licence to sell Handyman franchises in an area designated Handyman West, which included the western states. They claimed that Bricklin showed them figures indicating that Handyman America, Inc. possessed assets of $868,000, including cash of $75,000, and that Bricklin told them the chain of Handyman stores in Florida was profitable. On the strength of these figures, Fish, Hassel and Bair said that they entered into a June 5, 1964 agreement with Bricklin to sell Handyman franchises in the western states. "Written statements (provided by Bricklin) were not true and accurate sales figures for Florida stores, but were entirely fictitious." their court claim said. " . . . In fact true and accurate sales figures for said stores were 100 per cent to 400 per cent less than those represented." The claim also alleged that Handyman possessed "no assets except derived from these plaintiffs and persons similarly situated." It alleged that Handyman could supply none of the services it promised in the June agreement. Fish, Hassel and Bair sought combined damages of $156,000, plus court costs.

On November 4, 1964, Lawrence Fish of Short Hills, New Jersey, launched an action in District Court in New Jersey against Handyman America, Inc., Malcolm Bricklin, Albert Bricklin, and other officers of Handyman. Fish alleged breach of contract, fraud and misrepresentation. He alleged that in February, 1964, while he was a management official of the J.C. Penney hardware chain, Malcolm Bricklin, Albert and other Handyman officers told him during meetings in Florida that the Central Florida "test" licence for Handyman — the first licence that Handyman had attempted to develop — was a profitable one. Fish alleged that in March, 1964, Malcolm Bricklin sent him "certified" figures showing that the Central Florida licence had retained earnings of $55,796.89 as of October 31, 1963. The same month, Bricklin presented Fish with figures showing that Handyman had assets of $868,000. On the strength of these figures, Fish said he agreed to accept a position with Handyman, leaving his job with J.C. Penney, and that he also purchased shares in a Handyman subsidiary. Fish said that in August, 1964, he discovered that the figures presented to him by the Handyman officers were false. "Rather than having retained earnings of $55,796.89 on October 31, 1963, as represented, the Central Florida licence had a deficit of $130,500.48. The stores in the Central Florida licence, rather than enjoying sales of $533.19 to $6,756.56 a month as represented, did in fact have sales ranging approximately 100 per cent to 400 per cent less than the figures as represented . . . Rather than being profitable operations, the stores in the Florida licence were not profitable." In addition, Fish alleged, Malcolm Bricklin mailed him a purported balance sheet for Handyman and two subsidiaries in July, 1964, which showed that the companies had shareholders' equity of $692,745, cash of $195,000 and negligible current liabilities. Fish alleged that he subsequently discovered that the balance sheet was "deliberately misleading and false and failed to show outstanding indebtednesses of the corporate defendant, did not indicate property assignments against such indebtednesses, and misrepresented stockholders' equity." Fish sought damages of slightly over $1 million.

In December, 1964, Robert Kohlman of New Orleans filed suit in District Court in Orlando, Florida, against Handyman America, Inc.,

Malcolm Bricklin, Albert Bricklin and other officers of Handyman. Kohlman alleged that he had been defrauded. Kohlman alleged that he had bought a Handyman Southwest licence in April, 1964, on the strength of figures given to him by Malcolm Bricklin and other Handyman officers, which indicated that the Handyman operation in Florida was a profitable one. Kohlman alleged that he later discovered that the figures shown to him were false, and that Handyman and the individual defendants knew when they showed him the figures that "the Handyman operation was precarious, that it was having difficulty in meeting its obligations . . . " Kohlman asked for damages of $1.2 million.

Curiously, Kohlman had sought the advice of Philip Zeidman, a Virginia marketing analyst, before he invested in a Handyman franchise. In a lengthy letter dated May 19, 1964, Zeidman presented an analysis of the Handyman operation. He noted that the idea of franchises had caught on in the U.S. He also noted that Handyman intended to adapt new techniques such as computer purchases and central storage to the hardware business. But Zeidman questioned Bricklin's projections of how big Handyman would grow. "Mal Bricklin's figures are absurd," Zeidman wrote. "Bricklin's figure of 10,000 stores ultimately is so grandiose as to throw doubt on the whole idea." Zeidman admitted that, "It is possible, of course, that I am all wrong; this may be the greatest merchandising idea since vending machines . . . " But he raised other doubts, based on figures provided by Handyman. "Are the expenses being underestimated, and the profits therefore overestimated? Is too much being skimmed off?" Zeidman also noted "a tendency in the operation to be greedy; this could be fatal." He urged Kohlman to examine the Handyman figures closely, and then, "when all the figures are in, forget all the numbers and just smell it. If it smells good, go ahead." Kohlman, in 1964, was in the position the New Brunswick government would be in in 1973. Kohlman decided it smelled good. Eight months after Kohlman sniffed, he was taking Bricklin to court.

Lawrence Fish, Robert Kohlman, Vernon Fish, Harold Hassel and James Bair would be awarded judgments by courts in Florida and California, but they wouldn't collect. On April 6, 1965, Handyman America, Inc., Handyman Properties, Inc. and Handyman of Central Florida, Inc., filed for bankruptcy in U.S. District Court in Orlando, Florida. Handyman had announced it would appeal the judgments on the lawsuits, but the bankruptcy halted those proceedings. Handyman listed debts of $864,510.28 and assets of $237,906.29 in its bankruptcy petition. At the time of the bankruptcy, Bricklin was no longer associated with Handyman. He bailed out of his 147-store empire (in fact, there were 16 stores, including 14 in Orlando) in early 1965, after the lawsuits were launched. His later claim that he sold his Handyman interest for $1 million after taxes puts a burden on the imagination. Lawrence Fish, who left a position with J.C. Penney in 1964 to join Handyman, would laugh at Bricklin's claim. Fish reached a settlement with the Bricklins after the bankruptcy proceedings. The Bricklins and Samuel Pinsky, another Handyman officer, agreed to pay $2,000 to Fish. Fish received a down payment of $500 and monthly payments of $250 from Samuel Pinsky, Albert Bricklin and Malcolm Bricklin, the boy millionaire. Curiously, Albert Bricklin listed himself as one of the creditors in the Handyman bankruptcy proceedings. Albert claimed that he was owed $8,000 for the sale of eight Handyman franchises at a fee of $1,000 for each franchise. Another creditor of Handyman was Ben Bricklin, to whom Handyman had been making loan repayments.

In 1965, while Handyman was collapsing, Bricklin left Orlando for Philadelphia, the city of his childhood. Albert Bricklin had operated a fur store in Philadelphia when Malcolm was growing up. When Bricklin returned, he was twenty-six and looking for something to do. He decided to become a consultant. He formed a consulting agency called Universal Marketing, Inc., which consisted of himself (he was president), and began to cast around. A relative who lived in Bricklin's old Wynnefield neighborhood put him in contact with David Rosen, a middle-aged Wynnefield native who distributed pinball and vending machines. Rosen took Bricklin to Italy to investigate the possibilities of distributing an Italian-made jukebox, called the Cine Box, which played records and showed a short film at the same time. In Italy, Bricklin met officials of Innocenti, a company that manufactured scooters. Bricklin wanted to become their U.S. distributing agent. The company, in fact, had a stock of Lambretta scooters in storage in New York, and had never been able to sell them. Innocenti agreed to provide Bricklin with a salary and an expense account while he attempted to sell the scooters. Bricklin quickly translated the expense account into a Rolls Royce, from the trunk of which he would sell scooters. Rosen, who had taken Bricklin to Italy, returned to the U.S. to work on the distribution of Cine Boxes. It would be useless work. The Cine Boxes wouldn't catch on, and Rosen would drop them after suffering a heart attack. Bricklin fared better with his scooters, many of which he persuaded the New York Police Department to buy for its Central Park patrols.

Bricklin settled into the importing business. After selling the Lambrettas, he became a distributor for Rabbit scooters, manufactured by Fuji Heavy Industries of Japan. At the same time, he resurrected his old franchise system, which he had developed with the Handyman stores. Using his Rolls Royce for an office, Bricklin sold Rabbit franchises to service station owners and used car lots in the Philadelphia area. For a franchise fee, buyers would receive a Rabbit sign and a stock of Rabbits, which they could sell or rent. They would also receive parts and service for the lightweight bikes. Several of the dealers would claim later that Bricklin didn't deliver all the Rabbits they paid for, and many would complain that they couldn't get service when their scooters broke down. But while the complaints were developing, Bricklin was moving out of the scooter business.

Fuji also manufactured cars, called Subarus, but the company had never attempted to break into the small-car market in the U.S. Fuji wasn't prepared to undertake safety modifications required by U.S. import regulations. It also wasn't prepared to battle with the German-built Volkswagon, which dominated the U.S. small-car market. Bricklin, who had been eyeing Fuji's cars for some time, made an interesting discovery: he uncovered a U.S. import rule to the effect that anything weighing under 1,000 pounds isn't a car — and thus doesn't have to conform to government safety regulations. Fuji's smallest car, the Subaru 360, weighed 965 pounds. Persuaded, Fuji gave Bricklin distribution rights for the little Subaru.

Bricklin formed a partnership with Harvey Lamm, a young man his own age who had been putting in time in a family furniture business in Philadelphia. Together, they formed Subaru of America, Inc., and began to sell. Operating from a Philadelphia showroom and office, they peddled the tiny Subarus on a franchise basis to service station owners and used car lots throughout Pennsylvania. The car's selling points were a cheap price and reported high gas mileage, and they caught on quickly. With sales rising, Bricklin and Lamm obtained bank financing and began to expand the Subaru franchise network into other states. The pattern of Bricklin's earlier ventures asserted itself. He hired his mother, Gertrude, as a bookkeeper. He hired his brother-in-law, Michael Jonas, to supervise the construction of a new office building, the first of Bricklin's legendary offices. The building included, among other extravagances, seven closed-circuit television screens for Bricklin. With sales continuing to expand, Bricklin purchased a private plane, a helicopter and a yacht, which he floated off Newport Beach in California, where he was beginning to expand the Subaru network. At the height of sales, *Consumer Reports,* a U.S. consumers' magazine, released studies that said the Subaru 360 was the most unsafe car in the U.S. The car's sales plunged. Dealers, who were becoming unhappy anyway with a lack of service, refused to carry the car, and banks, which had provided Bricklin with backing of nearly $1 million while the Subaru network was expanding, began to press for repayment.

In desperation, Bricklin persuaded Fuji to make modifications to a heavier car, the Subaru Star, so it could be imported to the U.S. To develop sales among dealers who had perceived parts and service weaknesses in his Subaru 360 operation and who saw the same problems with the Subaru Star, Bricklin developed a parts distribution proposal that was amazingly like the central warehouses he had proposed as the core of his Handyman chain. He would establish "Subaru hospitals" in central locations to provide parts and repair work for Subaru owners. But, with his heavy debts, Bricklin couldn't find a bank to finance his plan. He cast around for private investors and finally made connections with Rusar Corporation, an investment company operated by the New York-based Koffman family. The Koffmans invested under terms that would push Bricklin out of the Subaru operation. In 1971, Bricklin settled out of Subaru for an undisclosed amount of money and 1,000 of the unsaleable Subaru 360s. By this time, he was developing other plans.

The Subaru 360s had been wasting in storage for several months, and Bricklin had been wondering what to do with them. While still with Subaru of America, he had built a small race track near the Subaru office, on which he would sometimes race a little Subaru. Bricklin decided that other people might want to race the cars. He formed a new company, FasTrack International, Inc. (the Subaru racetracks, which he could now see stretching across the U.S., would be called FasTracks) and began to look for investors in his racetrack scheme. For a franchise fee of $25,000, investors would receive 10 stripped-down Subarus and some racer's uniforms, which they could rent to amateur racers. The profits to investors, according to a prospectus that Bricklin quickly worked up, would be in the range of $100,000 a year.

At this point, Bricklin was full of ideas, but short on money. He founded another company, FasTrack Leisure Land, Inc., to attract investors. A spin-off from his racetrack idea, FasTrack Leisure Land would develop franchises for resorts across the U.S., on which Americans with money could vacation and, if they wanted, race Subarus. All that Bricklin needed was investors. He found one. Leon Stern, a Pompano Beach businessman, agreed to form a partnership with Bricklin to develop leisure land resorts. In 1971, Stern transferred to FasTrack Leisure Land, Inc. a resort property he owned in the Poconos, as part of the partnership agreement. Stern would soon discover that Bricklin, who was spinning frantically with ideas, didn't have time to devote to the proposed resorts. In fact, Bricklin was using Stern's property for other activities. In 1972, Stern would launch a breach-of-contract suit against Bricklin. Stern would assert in court that Bricklin had used his land title as security for large loans from Philadelphia banks, which were used to finance other activities. In December, 1974, a Philadelphia District Court jury would agree with Stern. It would order Bricklin to pay damages of $2.3 million to Stern.

Bricklin's other activities were the development of a car. He had hired Bruce Meyers, a design maverick and creator of the fibreglass-body dune buggy, to design a safe body for the Subaru 360s that Bricklin hoped to race. Bricklin realized that one problem with putting the Subarus on racetracks would be heavy body damages. He instructed Meyers to develop a plastic body, even a clip-on body that could be simply replaced when it wore out. Bricklin also began to ask questions about acrylics. His FasTrack companies weren't going anywhere, and he needed something to sell. Why not cars? If he could make a cheap car body, Bricklin thought, he could make a cheap car. The car would be a compact. Bricklin had an idea that he would sell it to Third World markets. Bricklin had a whole world of markets to develop. Franchise fees for the picking.

Bricklin formed two car companies. General Vehicle Inc. and Bricklin Vehicle Corporation were incorporated in 1971 in Delaware, a state with company laws so lax that companies incorporated there are not even required to file annual returns. At the same time, Bricklin instructed Meyers, his designer, to begin work on a new car design. Bricklin gave Meyers instructions to design an inexpensive, four-cylinder car. The car, Bricklin thought, should have gull-wing doors — an idea that appealed to him. Meyers went to work, but he was unable to design the car Bricklin had in mind (Bricklin would complain later that all of Meyers' proposals looked like the Datsun 240Z). In early 1972, Bricklin replaced Meyers with Marshall Hobart, another designer. Hobart made drawings, based on Bricklin's concept of a car, and in mid-1972 the drawings were turned over to Dick Dean, a custom car builder in southern California. Using a small shop in the Newport Beach area, Dean pinned Hobart's drawings to a wall and went to work. By late 1972, he would have constructed a prototype car.

But even as Dean worked, the very nature of Bricklin's car was changing. For one thing, the original intention to use a four-cylinder Opel engine was abandoned. Bricklin believed he had a deal with Chrysler for some six-cylinder engines, and so the prototype became a six-cylinder car — resulting in an overall weight change to 2,200 pounds from the proposed 1,600 pound car Dean was instructed to build. Other components for the car were hand-picked: the rear suspension was from a Datsun 510; the front brakes were a combination of brakes used in the Opel, the Datsun and the Toyota; a Chevrolet tilt steering wheel was installed; and mag wheels and tires were picked from a speed shop.

"I was the fabricator," Dean would say in a later interview, "although I don't try to take credit for the design. That was preconceived by Malcolm Bricklin, not so much the styling as the concept . . . he was insistent on the gull-wing doors from the beginning." Dean thought the doors were a blunder.

Dean's prototype was completed in December, 1972. The car, of course, was a design concept, such as any hobbyist with an imagination might put together in the back yard. It was not a production model. Nonetheless, Bricklin took publicity shots of the prototype, made a short movie, and began to look for investors and a place to build his car.

Whether the Poconos land title played a role, Bricklin was able in late 1972 and early 1973 to raise an estimated $950,000 from banks in Philadelphia and New York for his car project. The largest investor was the First Pennsylvania Bank, which provided a loan of $500,000 on the recommendation of bank president John Bunting, who had built something of a reputation for the First Pennsylvania Bank in the venture field. As security on portions of his loans, Bricklin pledged his remaining shares in Subaru, and provided personal guarantees. Bricklin had earlier loans outstanding from the Subaru period, totaling roughly $1 million. In other words, when he began in late 1972 to look for a place to build his car, he brought with him a single prototype and debts of $2 million.

Using his loans, Bricklin rented a building at Livonia, near Detroit, and hired a handful of production personnel from the Detroit automobile industry to make a production model of Dean's prototype, a process that Bricklin assumed would take about as long as was required to put together the prototype. With research under way, Bricklin ran into a special deal with American Motors, which was eager to sell 3,000 V-8 engines. The engines had been intended for use in a sports car that American Motors was developing to challenge the Chevrolet Corvette, but the company decided to abandon the plans. Bricklin picked up the engines. Suddenly the Bricklin car was to be an eight-cylinder vehicle. Bricklin began to make plans for producing cars in the spring of 1973. He settled upon a March date for production. All he needed was a plant in which to build the cars, and dealers to sell them. He began to canvas for dealers. At the same time, he hired Jack Reese, a sales executive who had worked for Renault at a company plant at St. Bruno, Quebec, to develop a Bricklin dealership organization. Bricklin and Reese, using only Bricklin's short film of a car, would persuade half a dozen dealers in the winter of 1972-1973 to place advance orders for about 2,000 Bricklin cars. To validate the orders, Bricklin and Reese obtained letters of credit from the dealers' banks. The letters would provide a line of credit to the dealers (a standard practice, which reflects a dealer's credit position with banks) for the purchase of Bricklin cars. With dealers falling into place, Bricklin began to look for a plant. Reese had informed him that Renault intended to close its eight-year-old plant at St. Bruno, near Montreal, in the spring of 1973.

In late 1972, Bricklin and Joe Rose, a certified public accountant with the well-connected New York accounting firm of Isola, Rose and Patone, which had performed work for Bricklin while he was with Subaru, approached the Quebec government to inquire about the Renault property. The Quebec government was anxious to find a new operator for the plant. Bricklin brought with him his film of a prototype car, several bank letters of credit for dealers, some projections of the number of cars he would build, and a schedule that said he would be in production by March, 1973. All he needed was money and a plant. He proposed that he would build cars at St. Bruno if the Quebec government would provide financing of about $7 million, in exchange for a position as a minority (40 per cent) shareholder in the project.

The Quebec government was interested enough to dispatch Jean de Villers, a senior Renault executive who was on a retainer from the government to find a new plant operator, to Philadelphia in January to investigate Bricklin's background. De Villers found that Bricklin was living well. Bricklin possessed, for example, a Rolls Royce, a Corvette and a Lamborghini. De Villers wasn't familiar with the Stern lawsuit, which had been launched in early 1972. It was still in the courts. De Villers returned to Quebec in late January with a report that Bricklin was a recognized promoter, but that his management ability was not impressive. De Villers recommended that the Quebec government turn down Bricklin's proposal, which it proceeded to do. Guy Saint-Pierre, Quebec's minister of industry and commerce, would say later that Quebec wasn't prepared to accept a minority position while putting up most of the capital for Bricklin. "If the business went well, they would make a fortune, and if it folded we would take all the blows," Saint-Pierre would say.

With the Quebec negotiations collapsing in late January, Rose contacted Leon Klein, a Montreal accountant and small-time promoter with whom Rose had dealt in the past. Klein, a large, garrulous man with a hanging stomach, had once ventured into the health food business, but his chain of stores in the Montreal area had collapsed. Now he ran a general accounting service out of an office on Van Horne Street, while keeping an eye out for a big chance. Did Klein have any ideas for Bricklin?

As a matter of fact, yes. Klein and his brother, Sam, had attempted recently to interest the New Brunswick government, among others, in a perfect water-pump filter they had developed. (Leon and Sam had proposed to call themselves Commandment Industries Ltd. Their motto would be The Eleventh Commandment — Thou Shalt Not Pollute. However, the federal department of regional economic expansion and the New Brunswick government declined to bite, and, with no financing forthcoming, the Kleins had put their perfect filter on a back burner). Klein had carried on his pump filter negotiations with New Brunswick Multiplex Corp., a federal-provincial development agency with offices in Saint John. Klein told Rose he would contact Multiplex about the Bricklin car. It was Klein's big chance. He would soon be hired by Bricklin. Eventually, Klein would rise to the position of comptroller of Bricklin's U.S. companies. Among other things, Klein would confide to Bricklin that he was a personal friend of Prime Minister Trudeau.

Chapter 3

THE MULTIPLEX NEGOTIATIONS

Government development agencies operate in a nether world of leads and half-leads, where business proposals and hokum schemes mingle and sometimes merge. Because the agencies are in the business of providing risk or venture money, often where banks fear to tread, they entertain a gamut of people in their offices: legitimate businessmen, promoters of all shades, and the occasional charlatan. New Brunswick, a small province with chronic high unemployment, has seen its share of charlatans. When the province's development officers aren't engaged in such harmless pursuits as the clipping of contacts from the pages of the *London Financial Times* or the preparation of lengthy, jargon-burdened studies, they are actively searching for business. And, of course, when the telephone rings, there is no telling who will be on the line.

"A call from Mr. Klein in Montreal . . ."

Richard Fletcher, the general manager of New Brunswick Multiplex Corp., picked up the telephone. Leon Klein's voice came over the line. Klein had a client who was considering the possibility of establishing a car-assembly line plant in New Brunswick. Was Multiplex interested?

Fletcher, a New Brunswick-educated economist in his late thirties, would insist later that he was initially skeptical about the Bricklin project. He would say he became more interested when he discovered that Bricklin intended to assemble his car with off-the-shelf parts. Regardless, he agreed to a meeting with Rose, Bricklin's accountant, in Montreal in early March. Klein, thus encouraged, wrote a letter in early February to the federal department of manpower at Halifax, requesting a grant to train New Brunswick workers to make cars. The letter was written on a Bricklin Canada Ltd. letterhead. Bricklin Canada Ltd. wouldn't be incorporated for another three months. The manpower department eventually would provide $300,000 to Bricklin to train workers.

On March 9, 1973, Fletcher, the Multiplex official, met with Joe Rose at the Chateau Champlain in Montreal. According to a Multiplex memorandum of the meeting, Rose told Fletcher that Bricklin intended "to build a factory to produce Plexiglass DR reinforced (acrylic) sports car bodies and assemble with a Dodge Duster or American Hornet power package." According to the memorandum, Fletcher was told that Bricklin had ordered a 300-ton press from Danby Press of Chicago for moulding body parts. Including the press, Bricklin had ordered $500,000 worth of equipment from Danby, according to the memorandum. (In fact, Bricklin didn't receive a body-moulding press until March, 1974. The press received by Bricklin was ordered from ECM of Texas, after Bricklin received New Brunswick financing). "Time is of the essence," said the March 9 memorandum, "as each month that the company is not in products costs the company $20,000 in overhead expenses. They will require an extensive manpower training program on assembly lines. This could be done in a rented building while the main plant is being built."

Fletcher would say he was still skeptical after his meeting with Rose, but he agreed to a March 14 meeting with Bricklin at Montreal's Airport Hilton. Bricklin brought Rose and some other key personnel to the March 14 meeting: George Rahman, 48, formerly with Chrysler of England, who would act as senior vice-president of Bricklin's U.S. operations before leaving in disgust in 1974; Jack Reese, 49, formerly with Renault and Mercedes Benz, who would construct Bricklin's U.S. dealer network before he was fired by Bricklin in 1975; Richard Vollmer, 49, a member of the team that developed the Ford Mustang, who would become Bricklin's director of manufacturing; and, Jean de Villers, formerly of Renault, who had investigated Bricklin on behalf of the Quebec government. By this time, Bricklin and de Villers had an understanding. By June, the understanding would blossom into the hiring of de Villers as president of Bricklin's Canadian operations.

After the March 14 meeting, Multiplex prepared a bulky preliminary report that was not skeptical. It was completed in three weeks. Whole sections of it were lifted without examination from a Quebec government report on the Bricklin project. Investment figures and production projections were provided solely by Bricklin. Multiplex ran the investment figures through a computer to establish the projected operating costs for Bricklin Canada Ltd. The result was a return on investment of 18 per cent over 20 years. The projected return on investment would be 29 per cent if Bricklin received a DREE grant. Multiplex quickly forwarded its report to DREE in support of a grant for Bricklin.

The Multiplex report is worth recounting in detail. It gives an idea of Bricklin's sales pitch at the March 14 meeting, since the figures and projections in the report were provided solely by Bricklin. Also, the Multiplex report was the only feasibility study undertaken by the New Brunswick government before it decided to finance Bricklin.

According to the report, Bricklin would use a DREE grant to assemble cars in a vacant plant in Saint John's Grandview industrial park (the plant, which formerly housed a brush industry, was suggested by Multiplex). According to the report, Bricklin needed an investment of $5.5 million to begin production (this figure included $250,000 for land, $2 million for a building, $2 million for machinery and equipment, and $1.2 million for moulds, tools and dies).

According to the report, Bricklin intended to build a "sporty car" to compete with such cars as Ford's Mustang, the Chevrolet Camaro and the Pontiac Firebird. A black-and-white photograph in the report verified the existence of Bricklin's prototype, with its gull-wing doors raised. According to the report, Bricklin intended to be in production by September, 1973. He intended to sell 10,000 cars in his first year of operation, 18,000 in his second year, 27,000 in his third year, 30,000 in his fourth year, and 32,000 in his fifth year.

The report said that Bricklin intended to sell his New Brunswick-built cars to his U.S. marketing companies for $2,172 apiece. This price, he said, would allow the New Brunswick factory a small profit. He intended to retail his cars in the U.S. for under $5,000 each.

The report described General Vehicle Inc. as the parent company of the proposed operation, and listed GVI's shareholders as Malcolm Bricklin (1.1 million shares), his sons, Craig, Kevin and Mark (100,000 shares each), and Pit and Co. of New York (60,000 shares). But the report didn't include a balance sheet to show the value of the shares. Bricklin had issued the shares for one cent apiece.

The report contained a description of executives who were said to be on Bricklin's payroll. The descriptions were lifted wholesale from an earlier report prepared for the Quebec government. They were not altogether accurate. Malcolm Bricklin, for example, was described in the report as having "considerable experience with manufacturing and marketing transportation vehicles," although his only manufacturing experience at the time was in the building of his prototype.

The report contained no car specifications. There were none. The report did not say whether the technology of bonding fibreglass to acrylic, to make the Bricklin bodies, was proven. It was not.

The report contained one set of figures that had impressed Multiplex, and would later impress DREE. According to the figures, Bricklin had presold over 2,500 cars to U.S. dealers. The figures were backed up by various letters of credit issued by U.S. banks to several car dealers, indicating the banks' willingness to finance the purchase of Bricklin cars by the dealers. The letters provided, in total, for dealer financing of $5.8 million. Bricklin represented the letters to the government officials as "irrevocable letters of credit." Of course, the letters reflected only on the credit status of the dealers, not Bricklin. And, of course, they hinged on whether Bricklin could deliver the cars.

The Multiplex report suggested a DREE grant of $4 million for Bricklin, based on a federal grant formula that takes into account the number of jobs to be created (it was estimated that Bricklin would employ an initial 264 workers) and eligible company assets.

With its report completed, Multiplex pursued the Bricklin negotiations at the federal level. Fletcher sought a meeting with R. D. Love, DREE's deputy minister. Garry Davis, a young Multiplex officer, flew to New York for further talks with Rose. With these initiatives, a meeting was arranged for April 18 at DREE's Laurier Avenue offices in Ottawa.

Bricklin brought his movie. He brought figures that showed he had presold a year's production of Bricklin cars. He brought Rahman, Rose, Vollmer, and de Villers. He brought T. Levy, an official of the First Pennsylvania Bank which had loaned $500,000 to Bricklin and was, of course, anxious for Bricklin to obtain money from other sources. Bricklin told the meeting the First Pennsylvania Bank had agreed to provide an additional $1 million, when a plant site was located. Rose talked about break-even points — Bricklin would break even on production at 800 cars a month. Bricklin said a decision was needed quickly if his company was to be in production by late August. According to a Multiplex memorandum of the meeting, J. P. Francis, an assistant deputy minister of DREE, promised to give the project "urgent attention."

But there were problems. To reduce the cost of production in Canada, Bricklin was anxious to obtain entry to the Canada-U.S. Auto Pact, a 1965 agreement that provides duty-free shipment of new cars and production parts between the two countries. Without an exemption under the pact, Bricklin would have to pay duties on parts and car shipments and then apply for duty rebates — an expensive, time-consuming process.

Ottawa's response to this was a worried frown. The federal department of industry, trade and commerce, which administers the Auto Pact in Canada, was worried that Chrysler, Ford and General Motors would be upset if Bricklin was allowed entry. DREE was worried that industry, trade and commerce would be upset if DREE applied pressure. But mostly, DREE was worried that Chrysler, Ford and General Motors would be upset if DREE gave a grant to Bricklin. So DREE hedged. (With all these worries, Ottawa was never able to screw its courage to the hilt and negotiate Bricklin's entry to the pact — a factor that Bricklin officials insist contributed to Bricklin's failure. In

April, 1974, a year after Bricklin's application for a grant, DREE provided a loan guarantee. Ottawa's hesitation was not due to doubts about the Bricklin car, which could have been justified, but to timidity at the thought of antagonizing the Big Three auto-makers).

With DREE vacillating, Multiplex went up the ladder for help. Fletcher approached Harry Nason, the province's deputy economic growth minister. Nason, a tall, thin man who seems to be all bones and horned-rim glasses, is one of Hatfield's most trusted advisers. Nason told Fletcher he would take Multiplex's concerns to Hatfield. Hatfield looked at the Multiplex report. He decided to raise the Auto Pact question with Allister Gillespie, the federal minister of industry, trade and commerce, and to pursue the question of a grant with DREE officials.

The Multiplex officials would plug away at the DREE negotiations for another month, but, lacking money of their own to invest, they gradually settled into the background. The project had gone above their heads.

Chapter 4

A GOVERNMENT DECISION

Hatfield believes that Canada's banks should play a role in regional development, by providing risk capital to under-developed areas like New Brunswick. The banks are, after all, an instrument of national policy. How effective can federal anti-disparities programs be if the banks, the federally-coddled banks, are permitted to discriminate against the have-not areas? It is virtually a truism that a new industry hoping to establish in New Brunswick can't get a bank loan without a government guarantee.

Hatfield also believes that New Brunswick, because it lacks the financial resources, must rely primarily on federal policies for development. He is a vocal supporter of DREE. But he thinks there are occasions when the federal government, for reasons such as expediency or neglect, doesn't act in the province's interests. When that happens, and when the bankers withdraw to their boardrooms, he thinks New Brunswick must take a leap on its own. This is why, for example, his government committed large funds to port development in Saint John (a federally-administered port) while Ottawa agonized over the effect on ports at Halifax and Montreal. It is one of the reasons, when DREE went into a soft shoe routine, Hatfield decided to invest in Bricklin.

There is another reason, harder to pin down. Hatfield is an intelligent man. He also has an openness about him that is rare in a politician, and rare anywhere. Some would call it naivete. In the case of Bricklin, some would call it gullibility. Hatfield is intrigued by life. His vacations don't take him to a beach in the Bahamas. They take him to Israel or Upper Volta. In his office, he is clearly the slightly-paternal premier of a small province, the son of a federal politician, Heber Hatfield, who founded a potato chip business at Hartland, in the St. John River Valley, and raised his children in a paternal fashion. But on his nights off, Hatfield is liable to be in a Montreal bar, digging life. He numbers writers and artists among his friends, and he ploughs his way through William Faulkner. Also, he has a weakness for style, and Hatfield was impressed with Bricklin's style. He was taken by the thought of building a sports car. For Hatfield, the Bricklin car was a cross between a development initiative and a glorious toy.

Hatfield raised the Auto Pact question with Gillespie, the federal minister of industry, trade and commerce, at a meeting in Ottawa in mid-May, 1973. Nothing came of it. Hatfield approached DREE the following week. DREE was still dodging on the grant application for Bricklin. Also, according to DREE, the Auto Pact question had moved no further.

Following the meetings with DREE, Hatfield met with Rose and Bricklin in Ottawa during the last week in May. According to Rose, the New Brunswick decision to invest in Bricklin, without DREE's help, had its beginnings at this meeting. Rose said in a later interview that Hatfield instructed him at this meeting to begin negotiations in Fredericton with Nason, the province's deputy economic growth minister. According to Rose, the Ottawa meeting was "the fore-runner" of the formal June, 1973, agreement between New Brunswick and Bricklin to build cars in New Brunswick. Certainly, according to documents and memoranda, the Bricklin officials proceeded in the next three weeks on the assumption that they would receive New Brunswick financing.

Hatfield had read the Multiplex report. It assumed that Bricklin was ready to go into production. All he needed, according to the report, was a plant and an initial investment. Presumably, Hatfield also believed that Bricklin was ready for production. New Brunswick had prepared no other reports. Hatfield would say in a later interview that he had also discussed the car project with John Bunting, chairman of the First Pennsylvania Bank, before a decision was made to invest in Bricklin. The bank, of course, had an interest in talking up the project. It had already provided loans to Bricklin.

After the late-May meeting between Hatfield and the Bricklin officials, events moved quickly. Bricklin dispatched Jean de Villers to Saint John to assess the plant in Grandview industrial park. De Villers would report that the plant was too small, but that it could be expanded if an adjacent parcel of land could be purchased.

On June 5, Rose hired Ian Whitcomb, a member of the Saint John law firm of McKelvey, MacAuley, Machum and Fairweather, to negotiate for a government loan and the plant. Rose also began the process of incorporating Bricklin Canada Ltd., the company that would assemble Bricklin cars. The same week, Albert Bricklin, Malcolm's father, arrived in New Brunswick to look things over. Albert had been running a vacation resort in the Poconos. Now he would help run a car company.

By the first week in June, the Bricklins and Rose were proceeding on the assumption that they had New Brunswick financing. Rose would say in a later interview that they had made their deal and were ready to go into business in late May. This approach created some consternation among provincial civil servants, who were processing Bricklin's application for a loan guarantee. The civil servants gained the impression that the Bricklin project had special status with the government. In coming months, they would be guided by this impression when they processed Bricklin applications for new financing. The normal process would be further complicated by Malcolm Bricklin's practice of personally floating his money requests with Hatfield, or even in the newspapers. In these circumstances, civil servants would not be inclined in coming months to go out on a limb and recommend a cut-off point for funds.

On June 5, for example, while Rose was engaging Whitcomb to represent Bricklin in negotiations for a loan guarantee and a plant, Alan Salke, another Bricklin official and long-time consultant on financial matters to Bricklin, was meeting with banks in New Brunswick "about financing the loan guarantee," according to a Multiplex memorandum dated June 5. The same day, according to another government memorandum, David Jennings, a middle-level economic growth department official with a reputation for competence in financial matters, was reported in a Multiplex memorandum to be "not overly enamored" with the Bricklin project. Jennings at that point was assessing the Bricklin loan application. According to the memorandum, which was prepared by M. G. Davis, a Multiplex official, "People at economic growth question the company's ability to sell the cars in the quantities indicated."

On June 7, Rose phoned Jennings, who was still processing the loan application. Rose told Jennings he wanted to speed up the loan. Bricklin needed the guarantee by June 11, Rose said. Jennings was hesitant. Economic growth wasn't ready to make a recommendation. As far as Jennings knew, DREE was still assessing Bricklin's grant application. Jennings put Rose off. The pattern would continue with later applications by Bricklin for money. The applications would make their way through the economic growth department, where they were dutifully analyzed. At the same time, Bricklin would be discussing his money needs with Hatfield. Civil servants would be aware of the discussions at a higher level while they were processing the applications. The result was a tandem-like process, full of uncertainty. Rose, who has a sense of humor, would later present Jennings with a set of magnetic worry balls, replicas of those fingered obsessively by Humphrey Bogart in the movie, *The Caine Mutiny.*

While the loan application was moving through the channels, another circumstance developed that was to leave a mark on the Bricklin project. Hatfield's government was fighting a June by-election in Saint John, called earlier in the spring to fill a seat made vacant by the death of George McInerney, a government member. Normally, governments in

New Brunswick can be expected to win by-elections — voters know a member can do more for them in government than in opposition. But the Saint John by-election had developed into an obviously close one, partly because of local support for Robert Higgins, the Opposition leader, and partly because of the tenacity of the campaign waged by John Turnbull, a city lawyer and the Opposition's candidate.

On June 21, five days before the by-election vote, the Montreal French-language newspaper, *Le Devoir,* broke the story of New Brunswick's negotiations with Bricklin. *Le Devoir* quoted a source to the effect that Quebec had lost an opportunity to revive the Renault plant at St. Bruno. Bricklin's car would be built in New Brunswick, with the aid of a $4 million DREE grant, the newspaper said.

Hatfield summoned several ministers and advisers to a meeting in Fredericton. Cabinet ministers and ranking civil servants later would insist the government had no intention of announcing the Bricklin project before the by-election. But now the news was out. Rumors and street talk were building in Saint John. Hatfield decided to go with an announcement. Arthur Parks, a special assistant to Hatfield, was sent to the offices of the New Brunswick Information Service, the government's publicity agency. Press releases were worked up. Hatfield collected the releases and went to Saint John to make the announcement.

On June 22, Hatfield told a hastily-assembled Saint John press conference that a car-manufacturing plant would establish in Saint John, with an initial investment of $6.5 million, and total investment of $9. million. The car company, called Bricklin Canada Ltd., would produce between 10,000 and 12,000 cars in its first year of operation, beginning in September. The cars would have unique safety features. The New Brunswick government would provide a loan guarantee of $2.88 million for working capital, and would purchase a majority of the company's shares for $500,000.

Hatfield was simply making the best of an uncertain situation. Given his choices, he would not have introduced such an unknown quantity so late in the campaign. Voters in rural New Brunswick will respond occasionally to eleventh-hour election announcements and gifts, but city voters are not so predictable. The only perceptible effect of Hatfield's Bricklin announcement was a move by borderline voters into the Liberal camp, insisting they wouldn't be bought.

On June 26, Saint John voted. Turnbull upset Dr. George Bate, the government candidate, by 86 votes.

Turnbull, whose grandfather invented the variable-pitch propeller, has an irreverent, inventive mind. He is a stocky, reputable lawyer with the persistence of a brush salesman and the instincts of a gumshoe. He also has a ringing voice and an outlandish laugh. In coming months, Turnbull would drive government members up the wall with an endless string of questions about Bricklin. He was certain the government had announced the Bricklin project in an attempt to pull the by-election from his sizeable jaws. The Saint John *Telegraph-Journal* would dub him the Liberals' hit man. Cabinet ministers would glower when he stood up in the House to ask questions. One day in 1975, Turnbull would get up and say that, after two years of digging around, he had finally found the hooker — Bricklin wasn't returning payments to New Brunswick for his cars. Then Turnbull would laugh his outlandish laugh. On that day, it is surprising that nobody on the government side reached for a gun.

On June 26, the day of the by-election vote, the New Brunswick government signed its first agreement with Bricklin. The government agreed to guarantee a loan of $2.88 million to provide Bricklin Canada Ltd. with start-up and working capital for the production of cars in Saint John. Malcolm Bricklin, through his U.S. companies, agreed to provide other working capital of $1 million. Before the agreement took effect, Bricklin was required to obtain supply contracts for major car components to ensure a year's uninterrupted production, and to provide evidence of admission to the Canada-U.S. Auto Pact.

Under the agreement, the government would purchase 51 per cent of the shares of Bricklin Canada Ltd. for $500,000 (the shares had no par value). As majority shareholder, the government would have access to the books of Bricklin's companies, and control over borrowing activities by Bricklin, and over company hirings and salaries. Remaining shares in Bricklin Canada Ltd. were assigned to General Vehicle Inc. in exchange for "manufacturing and design" rights that Bricklin had estimated to be worth $1 million.

Cars would be sold by Bricklin Canada Ltd. to Bricklin's U.S. companies for $2,200 each at Saint John — a price that was supposed to represent 125 per cent of the cost of materials and parts for the cars. Bricklin was not to produce cars elsewhere until he was able to reach and maintain production at 12,000 cars a year in Saint John.

The lengthy agreement did not define such critical terms as manufacturing rights, prototype testing, and engineering costs, for the simple reason that the New Brunswick officials did not know enough to define them. The New Brunswick officials simply assumed they were putting up money for car production in Saint John. They thought Bricklin was ready to manufacture cars. He was not. In fact, Bricklin needed money desperately to proceed with the initial engineering of the car. Even as the New Brunswick agreement was being signed, the

Detroit-based design firm of Visioneering, Inc. was pressuring Bricklin's U.S. companies for the payment of bills to cover Visioneering's initial engineering designs for the Bricklin car. The Detroit company had decided to withhold its drawings until payment was made. Shortly after the New Brunswick agreement was signed, funds were pulled from Bricklin Canada Ltd., the New Brunswick-financed company, to pay Visioneering. By July, a precedent was set for the use of New Brunswick funds to pay the cost of Bricklin's U.S. operations, although the funds were clearly intended to support production in Saint John. Until his companies collapsed in 1975, Bricklin would pull funds from New Brunswick to pay for his U.S. activities, including his expensive living habits. New Brunswick, not Bricklin, would pay for the development of the Bricklin car. The assignment of Bricklin Canada shares to Bricklin in exchange for manufacturing and design rights estimated by Bricklin at $1 million was simply a paper entry.

According to the agreement, the New Brunswick government had access to Bricklin's books, and broad control over the activities of Bricklin's companies. These prerogatives were not exercised. The government took the position initially that it didn't have the knowledge to operate a car-manufacturing company. The government didn't realize that Bricklin was in the same position. Because the government exercised no control, all of Bricklin's accounting records, including the Canadian records, were kept in the New York offices of Joe Rose for much of the production period. The government didn't see them. When Bricklin collapsed in 1975, the New Brunswick government would not know how much New Brunswick money had been diverted to Bricklin's U.S. companies.

Chapter 5

SETTING UP

On the weekend of June 24, 1973, while the by-election campaign in Saint John was winding to a close, Malcolm Bricklin flew with his three sons to Frobisher Bay in the Northwest Territories. Bricklin wanted Craig, Kevin and Mark to see the north country. Alan Salke, a long-time financial adviser to Bricklin (Salke would remain as Bricklin's consultant until early 1975, when the First Pennsylvania Bank would pressure him out of the car project), also made the flight. So did Jean de Villers. To help pass time on the flight, de Villers, who has a gentle French accent and the build of an ex-football guard, translated for Bricklin the story in *Le Devoir* of the Bricklin-New Brunswick negotiations. By the time the group returned to southern Canada, de Villers had been placed in charge of Bricklin's New Brunswick operations. In the summer of 1973, Bricklin and de Villers would attempt to build a car company. Their different approaches are instructive. Bricklin believed he would be in production by September. De Villers soon realized that Bricklin needed months of research work, competent management and another $20 million.

First, Bricklin. In July, with the ink still drying on his New Brunswick agreement, Bricklin moved from his mortgaged Philadelphia home to richer surroundings in Scottsdale, Arizona, a suburb of Phoenix. His new desert home was located in an enclave of adobe fortresses built by Hilton and rented to the rich. It came with room service. The ceilings had beams and there was a whirlpool bath on the patio. Soon there was a black servant named Bob, who was supplied with a station wagon.

Bricklin rented an office in Scottsdale's tallest building. He decorated the office in an Old Western motif. One wall consisted of false store-fronts, with each store-front bearing the name of a member of the Bricklin family. One section of the office was Bricklin's think tank. Here, Bricklin officials could sit with their coffee cups, gaze at a rug woven with a Bricklin 'B', and wonder if New Brunswick would give them more money. Bricklin, who had grown up in Philadelphia and Orlando, went western all the way. He put on a cowboy hat and hired his family. Albert, his father, was already president of Bricklin Canada Ltd. Gertrude, his mother, was hired as a bookkeeper (later, she would have the job, designated consumer relations, of personally answering customer complaints about the Bricklin car). Barbara Jonas, Bricklin's sister, was put in charge of public relations. She would edit the 'Brickline,' an employee newspaper. Michael Jonas, her husband, was named a legal adviser. Ben Bricklin, Malcolm's uncle, who had provided a loan to Malcolm when he was building Handyman, was attached to the Bricklin sales organization. Later, Bricklin would hire Colleen McCabe, who was to become his second wife.

Thus established, Bricklin set out to sell cars. With a commitment from New Brunswick, he could begin now to collect dealer franchise fees — a charge of roughly $5,000 per dealer that was intended to help support his U.S. sales operations. According to letters of credit shown to the New Brunswick government, Bricklin already had advance sales for more than 2,500 cars, but he intended to produce 12,000 cars in his first year, beginning in September. More dealers were needed. Throughout the summer of 1973, Bricklin directed his efforts towards lining up new U.S. dealers. Bricklin advertisements, prepared by the New York advertising agency of Lois Holland Callaway (creators of the ingenious Volkswagon-on-the-moon commercials of the '60s'), began to appear in U.S. newspapers. "For the past few months," one of the advertisements said, "you might have heard some enticing tidbits of information about an exceptional new automobile called the Bricklin, a car which has been under development for the past three years (In fact, Bricklin had only hit upon the idea of building a car two years earlier). Since the Bricklin is soon going into production, we are ready to start appointing dealers . . . We're looking for well-capitalized, well-established dealers . . . "

Gambling that it would obtain a lucrative account, Lois Holland Callaway worked up an entire Bricklin advertising campaign, built around the slogan, 'You'll think it is ahead of its time. We think it is about time.' Television commercials were prepared, featuring Malcolm Bricklin. The commercials were ingenious. In one of them, Bricklin approached a Bricklin car (a prototype, used in the entire Lois Holland campaign) with a large hammer. "It's the first car with an acrylic body ten times stronger than any steel or fibreglass body," Bricklin said. "Watch." Then he hammered the car four times. In another commercial, a camera dollied in on Bricklin: "On my right," he said, gesturing, "is a Datsun 240Z, worth $6,000. On my left (he blew a kiss) is a Bricklin, worth $5,000." The cars were gunned. They crashed into a wall. "The Datsun is now worth $3,900," said Bricklin. "The Bricklin is still worth $5,000." In yet another commercial, Bricklin crowed, "You know what turns people on the most? The doors. I know what turns me on the most. Those crazy doors." There were ten commercials in the series. Unfortunately, they were never used. Lois

Holland Callaway's advertising campaign was ready to go in October, but Bricklin wasn't in production.

Bricklin had prepared other forms of advertising, aided by Lois Holland Callaway. There were colored dealer brochures printed by Lebanon Valley Offset Printers, Inc. of Annville, Pennsylvania. The brochures were ingenious. Working with a single plate based on Bricklin's prototype, the printing firm used a color-over process to obtain pictures of cars in five different colors. The script in the brochures and in accompanying newspaper advertisements was Bricklin's. "There's more to the Bricklin than sexy doors," said one commentary. "Sooner or later," said another, "You're going to drive a Bricklin, which might prove to be the first great sexual experience of your lifetime." The advertisements and brochures made from Bricklin's prototype would form the basis for a massive dealership campaign in the next year. Dealers would pay for franchises on the strength of his brochures. Some of the dealers would wait two years for Bricklin to send them even one or two of the cars described in his brochures.

In the late summer of 1973, it began to dawn on Bricklin that he would have production problems. After the New Brunswick agreement was signed he had recruited engineers and production personnel to develop a manufacturing model at his rented plant in Livonia. He had assumed they could do the job in a matter of months. He was wrong. By August, it was evident that the conversion of Bricklin's prototype to a production model would be a lengthy and costly process. The reports from Livonia were not good. The Livonia engineers were scratching their heads and cursing the gull-wing doors, those crazy doors. They couldn't get them to raise. They couldn't get them to lock. The engineers were kicking the hand-fashioned acrylic bodies, which were too heavy for the car's springs and shocks. They were waiting for badly-needed parts, even making do with second-hand parts from American Motors. They had given up on Bricklin's initial intention of building a 2,200-pound car, and were struggling to bring the car's weight below 3,500 pounds. (They wouldn't succeed. The Bricklin car would weigh 3,800 pounds when it went into production). They had almost given up on Bricklin, and were chafing at his impatient demands to speed up the engineering process.

Bricklin had other problems. Although he had promised in his agreement with New Brunswick to raise $1 million in working capital in the U.S., he was having trouble warding off bank demands on his already-existing debts. He would not be able to raise the $1 million — that would be left to the New Brunswick government. In fact, far from raising money, Bricklin was attempting to stave off his bank debts with promises of royalties on his New Brunswick-built cars (By 1975

Bricklin would have pledged so many royalties on his car, that even if he had been able to build cars at the initially-projected cost, he would still be selling at a loss).

One of Bricklin's worrisome debts in the summer of 1973 was a loan of $170,000 due at the Lincoln Bank at Bala Cynwyd. In May, while he was negotiating with the New Brunswick government for financing, he had written to the bank in an attempt to have the loan extended. He had offered two alternatives for repayment: "First, if the loan is extended to September 1, 1973, it will be paid off by the company (Bricklin Vehicle Corp.). If the company is not in a position, then it will be paid from the proceeds of the sale of my house secured by the second mortgage you now hold. You will receive from the company $10 per car for the first 15,000 cars sold. If the loan is extended for the period of one year, the second mortgage as collateral is taken off. The collateral remains the company and my personal signature, similar to what First Pennsylvania has. At this point, you will receive $10 per car from the first 15,000 cars sold, plus 20,197 warrants of stock . . . " The bank's reply to Bricklin was a short one. "Delighted to hear everything is going well . . . advise you that alternative No. 1 is acceptable to the bank. We will look forward to repayment of our loan on September 1, 1973, from whatever source happens to be convenient to you." The bank wanted its money.

Faced with production and money problems, Bricklin continued to sell. It was what he knew how to do. Talking about a car that didn't yet exist, he managed to line up more than 200 dealers.

The September production date slid by. Bricklin began to revise his projections. The total investment before cars began to come off the assembly line would be $16 million, not the $6.5 million he had earlier projected. Production would begin before the year ended.

In early July, 1973, a week after he took charge of Bricklin's New Brunswick operations, Jean de Villers received a telephone call from Malcolm Bricklin. Albert Bricklin would be coming to Saint John to act as de Villers' assistant and to be a "seeing-eye dog" over the New Brunswick plant, said Malcolm. All right, said de Villers. A week later, Albert arrived in Saint John. Later, de Villers would remark glumly that Albert didn't see himself as an assistant to anyone.

With Malcolm Bricklin's permission, de Villers had hired half a dozen production workers from the former Renault plant at St. Bruno. These men were sent to Livonia for training, in preparation for a move to Saint John when an assembly line was established. On the suggestion of New Brunswick officials, de Villers had also decided to make use of an idle Government-owned plant in Minto for the production of body components, rather than wait for an expansion of the Saint John plant. At Minto, a small coal-mining town north of Fredericton, Bricklin workers would begin the task of manufacturing fibreglass-acrylic components for the Bricklin's body.

De Villers had understood that Robert Anderson, a Chicago-based plastics engineer with extensive experience in acrylics, would guide the production of body components at Minto. However, shortly after he went on the job, de Villers learned that Anderson had been released. There was no plastics expert. De Villers travelled to Minto to inspect the plant, and met Gerald Hodgeson, the fiftyish, English-born manager of a local fibreglass operation. De Villers hired him to replace Anderson.

Throughout the summer of 1973, de Villers and Hodgeson would attempt to establish a body parts operation at Minto. By the end of the summer, they would be throwing up their hands in frustration.

In early 1973, Bricklin had hired Visioneering, Inc., a Detroit-based design firm, to prepare engineering drawings for his car and to design tooling for car parts. But in July, Visioneering was ready to halt its work because Bricklin was falling behind on his bills. Visioneering had also decided not to release its engineering drawings until Bricklin caught up on his payments. To get the drawings, Bricklin had sprung funds from the New Brunswick-financed Bricklin Canada Ltd. Then, because Visioneering had put him on short notice, Bricklin had switched his design work to another Detroit firm, Hallowell Engineering. By this time, the delays were becoming costly.

The early designs prepared by Visioneering were sent to ECM, a Texas-based company that specializes in the manufacture of pneumatic presses. After the New Brunswick agreement was signed, Bricklin signed an agreement with ECM for a large vacuum-forming press (reported to be the largest press of its kind ever built) to be installed at Minto. ECM made a proposal to supply the remainder of the tooling that would be used at Minto, but Bricklin declined. ECM put Bricklin on a cash basis for the press, and he began to cast around for another company to do his tooling. The summer months had passed, and the delays were mounting. In desperation, Bricklin's production personnel decided to resort to temporary tooling — epoxy-coated tools that lack the strength of steel-tempered permanent tools — to get the Minto plant into operation.

By this time, Bricklin officials were spending more time in the air than on the ground. Production officials flew from Livonia (where the car was being designed) to Minto (where body parts were supposed to be built) to Saint John (where cars were supposed to be assembled). "Malcolm had not set up any lines of authority," de Villers would say later. "It was getting very expensive. It started to go bad. We had fifty or sixty people, and travelling expenses for all these people were very high. We had no product ready to go, and the costs were tremendous. And you know, Bricklin was not competent to judge. He had no knowledge of the detail. He still did not understand it."

De Villers had another problem. He couldn't get Albert Bricklin out of his hair. Albert was everywhere, fiddling with the fibreglass and gradually taking more and more management decisions onto himself. He began to overrule de Villers, and de Villers became fed up.

In early October, 1973, de Villers telephoned Malcolm Bricklin. He told Bricklin he wasn't happy with the deal. He wanted out. All right, said Bricklin.

Then de Villers telephoned Hatfield. He was prepared to meet with Hatfield. He thought the New Brunswick premier might have questions to ask. According to de Villers, the conversation went like this:

"Have you told the board (about the resignation)?" Hatfield asked.

"Yes," said de Villers.

"Okay, goodbye," Hatfield said.

Chapter 6

ATTEMPTS AT MANAGEMENT

By the winter of 1973, a pattern was set that would mark the Bricklin project until its end. Experienced production personnel, attracted by Malcolm Bricklin's talk of building a car outside the Detroit structure, would throw themselves wholeheartedly into the project and then gradually drift away in frustration over production problems, a maddening lack of management, and uninformed tinkering by the Bricklins. By early 1974, the problems would lead to open revolt among the production workers at Livonia. Albert Bricklin would be shuttled back to the U.S. amid threats of resignation if he were allowed to stay in New Brunswick. New production personnel would be brought onto the project, but still the problems would persist. The Bricklins ran the operation without understanding its problems. Production personnel, who understood the problems, were given no authority. The New Brunswick government, which had provided the financing, was simply not aware of what was going on.

With de Villers' departure, Morris (Morie) Adams was transferred from Livonia to Saint John to take temporary charge of the New Brunswick operations. Adams, a former production line supervisor with Chrysler, had a distinguished, 25-year automotive career behind him. He had been involved in the pioneering of air-powered tooling in the industry, and he had worked with acrylics. Caught up in the challenge of opening the Saint John plant, he would also manage to work with Albert Bricklin.

In December, 1973, Jack Hennessey was hired as vice-president and general manager of the New Brunswick operations, and Adams was placed in specific charge of the Saint John plant. Hennessey, a Canadian, had worked in management positions at Ford plants in St. Thomas and Oakville, both in Ontario, before taking an early retirement because of a heart attack. (The circumstances of his arrival in Saint John in January, 1974, were enough to give a man another attack. A car, sent by Albert Bricklin, was at the Saint John airport to meet Hennessey and Richard Vollmer, another Bricklin official, when they arrived on a late-night flight. They were taken over slushy streets to a Bricklin-rented apartment overlooking the Kennebecasis River, and Hennessey was bedded down on a settee. Throughout the night he tossed, driven to distraction by the snoring of a Bricklin accountant in the next bedroom. At five o'clock in the morning he got up to call a motel. The telephone was disconnected. He left the apartment and drove to a Holiday Inn which, luckily, had one vacant room.)

Coincident with Hennessey's arrival, Ian Watson, a young, English-trained accountant with Fram Canada Ltd., was hired as comptroller of Bricklin Canada Ltd. (Watson would last barely a year. He was naive enough to believe that Bricklin wanted him to establish coherent accounting practices and rational budgeting goals. Bricklin and his advisers wanted neither — such practices and goals would only impede their efforts to get money from New Brunswick.) When Watson arrived, he was presented with 3,500 shares in General Vehicle Inc. He believed the value of the shares would compound rapidly. He thought he had a foot-hold on a fortune. It was like getting in on the ground floor with General Motors.

Vic Scully, a thirty-year-old accounting supervisor with Chrysler Canada Ltd., was hired at the same time. He was given 1,500 shares in General Vehicle Inc. Recently separated from his wife, he thought of the Bricklin project as a new lease on life. Scully's career with Bricklin would follow a different course than Watson's. Scully was transferred directly to Livonia where he came under the tutelage of Joe Rose, Bricklin's financial advisor. Scully was later sent back to Saint John to be Rose's man in New Brunswick.

With the new hirings, there was a temporary rush of optimism in the Bricklin organization. Malcolm Bricklin took time off from his dealership campaign (a campaign that was taking him as far afield as Tulsa or Albuquerque or anywhere else he had a whim to visit when he woke up in the morning) to announce a January, 1974 start-up date, and to begin preparations for the showing of a Bricklin prototype at a Las Vegas car show in early February. But the new spirit didn't last. The production personnel at Livonia, Minto and Saint John — the only people with a true inkling of Bricklin's problems — were becoming more frustrated daily with the seemingly endless production problems.

First, Livonia. First, Herb Grasse, who deserves description. Grasse, a short, burly, bearded man, was in charge of designing a production model of Bricklin's car. He owned seven vehicles of his own, including a large van fitted with plush upholstery. A graduate of the Beverley Hills College of Design, Grasse had married Miss Playgirl of March, 1969. Shortly after the Livonia plant went into operation, it brimmed with a virtual calendar of former Miss Playgirls, hired as secretaries, much to the joy of the Livonia workers.

But by late January, 1974, there was little joy in Livonia. The Livonia personnel were becoming increasingly frustrated with the task of converting Bricklin's prototype to a production model. They couldn't solve the problem of the gull-wing doors. The door-raising mechanism wouldn't work. The door catches wouldn't work. The door itself was too heavy — it weighed 170 pounds. The Livonia workers resorted to a large air cylinder in an attempt to raise the door, but the cylinder took up space normally reserved for a driver's head. A German device, a combination motor and cylinder, was tried, but it burst into flames. The Livonia personnel suggested design changes, but Malcolm Bricklin refused. There were other problems. The windows leaked. There were critical delays in tooling. The plastics problems at Minto were becoming known.

Tom Monroe, a youthful, Ford-trained engineer, was attempting to construct a car chassis amid the confusion, altering the chassis as problems developed.

More changes were suggested to Bricklin, and he refused. The Livonia workers concluded that Bricklin didn't know what he was doing.

In late January, spurred on by George Rahman (a vice-president of General Vehicle Inc.) and Jack Hennessey, who realized soon after his arrival on the project that the Bricklins didn't understand the production problems, the Livonia personnel decided to take action on their own. Meetings were held. It was rumored that Studebaker, which had just gone out of business, was eager to sell the tooling for its Avanti sports car. It was rumored that efforts were being made to find a Canadian plant for the assembly of Avanti-type cars. The Livonia personnel decided to approach the New Brunswick government with a plan to build cars without Bricklin. They told the Livonia secretaries of their plans. The Livonia secretaries agreed to lock the engineering files and hold on to the keys.

Gerald Hodgeson, who was in charge of plastics production at the Minto plant, was making frequent flights to Livonia for advice in the winter of 1974. On one such flight in late January, he booked into a hotel and went out for a drink. He met a worker from the Livonia plant. After a few drinks, the worker spilled the plans for a revolt. It would take place the next day, which was a Friday. Hodgeson went back to his hotel room. He agonized. Like Hennessey, with whom he was developing a friendship, Hodgeson had been openly critical of the Bricklins in recent weeks, and he was gaining a reputation as something of a trouble-maker. He didn't want to become involved in the Livonia mess. He decided to go to sleep, but he was unable to do so. Finally, he decided to call Morie Adams, the manager of Bricklin's plant in Saint John, for advice. Adams insisted upon putting Albert Bricklin on the line, although Hodgeson by this time was seeing daggers at the thought of Albert. Grimacing, Hodgeson told Albert about the revolt. Albert was quickly on the phone to Malcolm.

Malcolm Bricklin flew to Livonia the next morning. Rahman, the leader of the revolt, was shuttled out of Livonia. Bricklin said he would be placed in charge of liaison with ECM, the Texas company that was building a press for the Minto plant. Shortly afterwards, Rahman's name disappeared from the Bricklin payroll. In fact, Rahman disappeared. Former associates say they don't know where he is. They say the last sign they have had of Rahman is his car, which was later discovered in an airport parking lot at Livonia. With Rahman gone, the Livonia revolt collapsed. Hatfield would hear rumors of the revolt and at a later meeting he would ask Bricklin about them. Bricklin, according to Hodgeson who was present during the exchange, would describe the revolt as a little misunderstanding.

With Livonia under control, Bricklin flew to Las Vegas where a Bricklin prototype would be unveiled on February 2. It would be the first showing of a Bricklin car, and Bricklin wanted to make an impression. The unveiling would take place at the Riviera Hotel, and would coincide with the annual convention of the American Automobile Dealers Association. Bricklin spent lavishly for the occasion. Paul Newman, the actor, was engaged to hang around the car and to have his photograph taken with potential Bricklin dealers. Racing driver Bobby Unser was also hired to make an appearance. The Bricklin hotel bill for the unveiling was roughly $10,000, excluding the costs of flying Bricklin guests to Las Vegas. Jack Reese, Bricklin's dealership organizer, signed 112 dealers during the show, but with the expenses involved, Bricklin hardly broke even. In Saint John two days later, Albert Bricklin told a local Lions Club meeting that Malcolm's "impossible dream" had become a reality. "To tell you the truth," Albert said, "I'm only helping him." Albert went on to describe the Bricklin as "one of the outstanding engineering achievements of the decade." In fact, Bricklin's production personnel at Livonia were still attempting to engineer the car. Albert showed pictures of the Las Vegas prototype to the Lions Club members, but when reporters approached for a look he quickly hid the pictures away, for reasons known only to Albert.

Meanwhile, the Livonia production personnel went back to their drawings, back to the wretched gull-wing doors, and back to their leaky windows. Their problems, however frustrating, were minor, compared to the problems in Minto.

By late January, 1974, Bricklin production personnel had begun to realize that Minto held the key to a production start-up. Hodgeson had been in charge of the Minto plant since August, 1973, with little to do but wring his hands, watch the fibreglass pile up, and make frequent flights to Livonia where the tooling was being designed. In January, Hodgeson was still waiting for vacuum-forming presses to arrive. The large body-moulding press was still under construction in Texas. With delays placing the entire project in jeopardy, production officials had decided to order temporary tooling for the Minto plant. Contracts for the tooling were placed in January with two companies, Engineering Tool and Machine (ETM), Inc., of Grand Ledge, Michigan, and Formative Products, Inc., of Detroit. The Bricklin officials hoped the tools would last a year. Then Bricklin could invest in permanent, steel-tempered tooling.

In early February, A. E. Jones, a former Ford engineer who had joined the Livonia staff, prepared a schedule for a move into production. The Livonia personnel were tired of Bricklin's constantly-changing start-up announcements. They wanted a rational schedule. Jones concentrated largely on Minto, where body parts production would have to begin before the Saint John assembly plant could go into operation. According to Jones' schedule, technicians would arrive in Minto on March 3 to install the large ECM press, which was designed for the production of Bricklin bumpers, fenders, and other large body parts. Jones projected that body parts production would begin on March 25. Smaller presses for the remaining body parts would be installed by April 15. C. A. Van Nortwick, another former Ford engineer, was placed in charge of finding the best process for bonding fibreglass and acrylic, the two components in the car body. Van Nortwick, like the rest of Bricklin's production personnel, believed this would be simply a task of finding the best adhesive among those recommended by Bricklin's plastics suppliers. By July, according to Jones' schedule, Van Nortwick was to have developed a process that would allow for the production of six car bodies an hour.

In February, the ECM press and the first tools began to arrive in Minto. Bricklin ordered acrylic materials from Rohm and Haas, a large plastics supplier, for the production of sixty car bodies. Then the problems began to develop. The temporary tools, which were epoxy-coated, lacked the strength of permanent steel-tempered tools. Many of them began to crack under pressure. Also, since they were specially designed, many of them wouldn't fit the standard small presses that Bricklin, shopping around, had bought off the shelf and installed at Minto.

There were worse problems. When the first acrylic arrived, Hodgeson and his small crew tested it. They found that the acrylic blistered at 150 degrees Fahrenheit. Since the surface temperature on the Arizona desert occasionally reaches 180 degrees, the material was not suitable. There was another problem. Hodgeson and his crew couldn't get fibreglass backing to stick to the few experimental parts they managed to make. Van Nortwick, the former Ford engineer who had been placed in charge of finding a bonding process, had developed several experimental processes. Van Nortwick had his own office in the Minto plant, and he had put up a sign — 'Director-Body Assembly' — on his door. He began to send out brief outlines of his suggested processes. Hodgeson and others, who resented his sign, looked at Van Nortwick's outlines and realized he was only guessing. The processes suggested by Van Nortwick were unproven, and proving them would be time-consuming and costly.

The unuseable Rohm and Haas acrylic left Bricklin with a dilemma. He would have to find a new type of acrylic, but, theoretically, that would require that he begin again the process of designing tools for the Minto plant, since the tools already shipped to the plant were designed for use with Rohm and Haas material. But Bricklin was already far behind in production and he couldn't afford further delays. Between them, Malcolm and Albert Bricklin decided to place an order with Swedlow, another plastics supplier, for more acrylic. They instructed the Minto personnel to adapt their tooling to the new material, which was substantially thinner than the Rohm and Haas material. This decision only plunged Bricklin deeper into a maze of problems. To make up for the thinness of the Swedlow material, the Minto personnel would have to add more layers of fibreglass to accommodate the tooling. The car weight problem, which the Livonia personnel were struggling to overcome, became even greater. But there was a worse problem. Hodgeson and his crew couldn't get fibreglass to stick adequately to the Swedlow material either. The plastics industry had succeeded in bonding fibreglass to acrylic in certain bathroom fixtures, but that was the extent of the technology. Similar bonding had never been accomplished in a car plant, and there was simply no way of knowing how factors such as the strength of the presses, humidity and expansion qualities of the materials would affect bonding. As the Minto personnel began to work with the acrylic, the enormity of the bonding problems slowly dawned on them. In coming months, the basic process of bonding fibreglass to acrylic would turn out to be the greatest problem at Minto. Technician after technician would experiment with bonding formulas and adhesive mixes without success. It would take months of searching and an incredible waste of time, money and materials before a workable method of bonding the materials was found. Bricklin would scrap the Swedlow acrylic, which was simply too thin for the Minto tooling. He would revert to Rohm and Haas acrylic which, for all its problems, fitted the temporary tooling. By then, Bricklin's start-up date would be pushed back another half-year. Even after a bonding method was found, there would be problems. The rate of materials scrap at Minto would continue to run at over 15 per cent, largely because of poor bonding. A major complaint of car buyers would be the poor fitting of Bricklin body panels.

By late February, 1974, Jack Hennessey was a man with problems. He had been with Bricklin less than two months and he was ready to resign. He had been hired as vice-president and general manager of the New Brunswick operations, but it was plain to him that Albert Bricklin didn't view him as a superior. Hennessey believed that Albert was attempting to downgrade his authority, by overruling him, by interfering, by intervening directly with people who were supposed to be under Hennessey. By February, Hennessey had begun to dislike Albert intensely. His feelings were reinforced by Hodgeson, who by this time was voicing the opinion that the Bricklins didn't know what they were doing. Hodgeson was still nursing a January quarrel with Albert over body costs. Albert had instructed him to prepare a cost study of components for a complete car body, and Hodgeson had come up with a figure of $440. Albert had indignantly ordered him to bring the cost down to $170, which Hodgeson knew was impossible.

Hennessey had other problems. It had become apparent that there would be costly delays, particularly at Minto, before production could begin. He sensed that nobody was in control of expenses, and that the whole project was proceeding without direction. Bricklin's accountants were in Saint John and New York. The development of a production model was being carried out at Livonia. The body plant was at Minto. The assembly plant was in Saint John. Bricklin officials were in constant flight between the different centres. Conflicts were developing. The Livonia personnel were becoming impatient with progress at Minto, and had begun to send a string of experts there to see what was happening. Hennessey attempted to develop organization charts and operating budgets, but it was impossible. For one thing, there was Albert, upsetting the organization charts by his very presence. Hennessey decided he wanted Albert out.

Hennessey took his concerns to a Bricklin budget meeting in Detroit in late February. He was prepared to resign if Albert wasn't removed from New Brunswick and if the Bricklins didn't accept Hennessey's plans for a reorganization. He had a three-page letter of resignation in his pocket. By this time, Hennessey knew what Bricklin's budget meetings entailed. They were, he would say later, no more than a recitation of who was on the personnel roster. The meeting was held at Detroit's Airport Hilton. Albert Bricklin was at the meeting, seated next to Malcolm. The others who attended the meeting were Joseph Rose, Vic Scully (Rose's protege), and Leon Klein, the former Montreal accountant who had joined the Bricklins when they received New Brunswick financing. Hennessey's re-organization plan was placed on the bottom of the agenda, but the group didn't get to it so a second meeting was arranged for the next morning. At the second meeting, over breakfast, Hennessey presented his plans to Bricklin. First, there was an ultimatum. If Albert wasn't removed from the New Brunswick operations, Hennessey would resign. Then Hennessey went on to describe the shake-up he had in mind. Every Bricklin employee would be assigned a particular job. Lines of authority would be established and followed. At this point, Joseph Rose entered the meeting, late. When he heard Hennessey's proposals, he threw his papers in the air. Eventually, he calmed down. After the excitement, Malcolm Bricklin drew a pyramid on a napkin. Then he said that Albert would be returned to Livonia from New Brunswick. Albert would be placed at the head of a three-man executive committee, which hadn't existed until that moment. However, nothing was done about Hennessey's reorganization plan. The plan would have placed more authority in the hands of production personnel. The Bricklins didn't intend to give up any of their authority.

Hennessey returned to the plants, where the production problems were no closer to a solution. He had made a permanent enemy of Albert Bricklin, and he wondered what that would produce. But now there was another problem that overshadowed the problem of Albert, and even overshadowed the production problems. The bills to Bricklin Canada Ltd. were backlogging. Bricklin was out of money.

Chapter 7

NEW FINANCING

Ian Watson, the young, English-born comptroller of Bricklin Canada Ltd., had some reservations about the Bricklin accounting system when he arrived in early 1974. For one thing, the New Brunswick government, which was the majority shareholder in Bricklin Canada, didn't even have a signing officer on the project to control expenses. Albert and Malcolm Bricklin signed cheques. So did Joseph Rose, the New York-based accountant and financial advisor to Bricklin. So did Leon Klein, the former Montreal promoter who had brought Bricklin and New Brunswick together and then had re-surfaced as a Bricklin accountant. Soon, Watson would have signing authority. But, to his surprise, nobody from the government approved any of the cheques before they were signed. The only direct government presence in the entire operation was young Stephenson Wheatley, an economic growth employee who had accepted an assignment that senior civil servants were falling over one another to avoid — that of full-time Bricklin observer. Wheatley only saw the Bricklin expense sheets at month-end, and the consensus among Bricklin officials was that Wheatley had no authority to do anything. According to Watson, Wheatley spent a lot of time suggesting that Bricklin personnel should bring their daily personal expenses into line with those in the civil service.

Watson had other reservations. Like Jack Hennessey, he believed that the Bricklin project lacked direction. There was no central control. Certainly, from an accountant's point of view, there was none. Bills were arriving in the Saint John office from every corner of the continent. Watson saw bills forwarded to Bricklin Canada for expenses incurred by Bricklin's U.S. companies before the New Brunswick company was even in existence. Many of the bills were going unpaid. By early 1974, Bricklin was avoiding his creditors. According to Bricklin sources, the Bricklin organization was frequently kiting cheques. It was common knowledge within the organization that Malcolm Bricklin was also dodging the U.S. banks that had invested in him. All sorts of excuses were being worked up to avoid progress meetings suggested by the First Pennsylvania Bank. Hennessey had to have a cast removed. Another key official had a stomach ulcer. Malcolm Bricklin had to fly to Albuquerque. Anything to delay the meetings.

Watson went to work. To create a system for warding off the Bricklin creditors, he ran the Bricklin bills through a computer to establish an "ageing analysis" — a record of which creditors had been waiting the longest for payment, and which could be expected to wait a little longer.

Then he devised an accounting system that was intended to reflect what was happening to money in the Bricklin organization — an accountant's equivalent of the organization charts that Hennessey had attempted, without success, to implement. Watson's system proposed six objectives which he hoped to have accomplished before the end of 1974. He wanted to segregate the burgeoning Minto costs from those for the Saint John plant, to give a clear indication of the cost of bringing the Minto plant to production. He wanted to generate accurate data for all transfer payments between Bricklin Canada Ltd. and Bricklin's U.S. companies — he was worried by the easy, largely unrecorded flow of funds to the U.S. companies. He wanted to establish a system by October, 1974, for the preparation of the Bricklin companies' annual statements for 1975. He wanted to have a system in place by October for determining actual production costs. He wanted a commitment from Bricklin management that 1975 financial objectives would be formulated by October, 1974, and he wanted management to actively assist in the preparation of manufacturing budgets for 1975.

Watson's system would have provided the precise sort of accounting controls that the New Brunswick government was to demand in 1975, after the government's investment in Bricklin had risen astronomically. But in 1974, nobody was interested in Watson's system. Wheatley, the government representative, was aware of Watson's proposals, but could do nothing about them. Joseph Rose, who kept all of Bricklin's books in his New York office, professed sympathy, but Rose knew that Bricklin couldn't afford to let the New Brunswick government know the full extent of problems at Minto. Rose knew the entire Bricklin project would be jeopardized if New Brunswick and Bricklin's U.S. investors were aware of the amount of money still needed before production could begin. So Watson's plan was pushed aside.

A bit subdued, Watson was introduced to the Bricklin method of budgeting. By February of 1974, Bricklin needed money badly. New Brunswick's initial investment, made in June, 1973, had been spent. Malcolm Bricklin had been unable to come up with the $1 million in working capital that he had agreed to raise when the 1973 agreement was signed. Expenses were mounting daily, and a production start-up was still far in the future. There was no money coming in. In effect, Bricklin was close to bankruptcy. The only possible sources of funds were the New Brunswick government, the First Pennsylvania Bank (which wasn't prepared to invest more money on its own), and the federal department of regional economic expansion (DREE), which had refused to provide a grant but was now considering New Brunswick representations to kick in a loan guarantee.

Watson began to travel to New York for money-raising meetings. Mindful of expenses, he would book into a cheap, housekeeping unit at the Gorham Hotel in New York. Wheatley, who attended the meetings as a government observer, would stay at the New York Hilton. Watson and Wheatley would go to Rose's office at 1345 Avenue of the Americas, where the money-raising meetings were held. Leon Klein, who also hung out at the Gorham Hotel, would be there. So would Vic Scully, the young accountant who had come under Rose's tutelage. Together, observed by Wheatley, the Bricklin accountants would make up their financial statements and projections, with an eye to persuading the New Brunswick government to invest more money. Rose, who negotiated with the government on behalf of Bricklin, referred to these statements and projections as "rolling cash budgets," or, occasionally, "selling statements." The purpose of the meetings was to strike upon an amount of money that the New Brunswick government could be persuaded to invest. By February, 1974, the Bricklin accountants knew they needed a lot of money.

Since 1973, the New Brunswick government had been seeking DREE involvement in the Bricklin project. DREE had refused to provide a grant, and the provincial representations had begun to centre around a loan guarantee. Malcolm Bricklin, under pressure from the First Pennsylvania Bank, was also making representations to DREE. By February, 1974, the money-raising efforts had developed into a complex poker game involving the New Brunswick government, DREE, and the First Pennsylvania Bank — and, clearly, New Brunswick held the weakest hand. DREE insisted that New Brunswick, which had a majority interest in Bricklin Canada Ltd. and hence the largest stake, should be prepared to make the largest investment. The First Pennsylvania Bank said it wouldn't raise its stakes without new security and without an initial move by New Brunswick, the prime investor. The provincial government knew that, for political and financial reasons, it had to find outside investors for Bricklin. Fed by Rose's "rolling cash" projections, the government also knew that Bricklin needed money immediately. With its back to the wall, where it would remain until New Brunswick put the project under in 1975, the provincial government took the first plunge on April 18, 1974. The remaining negotiations quickly fell into place. When the smoke had cleared, Bricklin had new, three-way financing. The New Brunswick government was left with virtually no security on its investment, and the First Pennsylvania Bank was grinning like a warm cat.

On April 18, with Bricklin barely holding off his creditors, the New Brunswick cabinet increased the government's loan guarantee to Bricklin from the original $2.88 million to $4 million. Shortly afterward, DREE announced a loan guarantee of $2.7 million. At the same time, the First Pennsylvania Bank agreed to provide a $3 million credit to Bricklin at four per cent over the bank's prime rate, for dealer financing. As security for its high-interest loan, the bank was assigned the right to car inventories and the right to Bricklin's accounts receivable, or book debts. The bank also took a second mortgage position on the Bricklin plants at Saint John and Minto, secured by the plants themselves, equipment, moulds, tools, machinery, furniture and parts inventories. The bank also received guarantees from General Vehicle Inc., Bricklin Vehicle Corporation, Bricklin Northeast Inc., and a personal guarantee from Malcolm Bricklin. The bank also received a further astonishing form of security. Bricklin Canada Ltd. (in effect, the New Brunswick government) was required to deposit $1 million in cash in a non-interest-bearing account with the First Pennsylvania Bank during the term of the agreement. The deposit was, in effect, an additional $1 million kick-in by New Brunswick to Bricklin. The province had to borrow the money at a going rate of interest, and then deposit it with the First Pennsylvania Bank at no interest.

Shortly after it struck this deal, the New Brunswick government transferred ownership of the Minto plant from the New Brunswick Development Corporation to the Industrial Finance Board, an agency within the economic growth department. The government did not disclose the transfer price. It considered the transfer to be simply a book entry, not representing a further investment in Bricklin. The economic growth department then proceeded to rent the Minto plant to Bricklin for $51,744 a year. Since the government was the majority shareholder in Bricklin, the government was its own tenant.

Hatfield and Paul Creaghan, New Brunswick's minister of economic growth, were jubilant when the three-way re-financing of Bricklin was announced. They hailed the new financing as evidence of outside confidence in the Bricklin project.

Shortly afterwards, the government faced its first questions about Bricklin in the legislature from the Opposition Liberals. During debate of his department's spending programs, Creaghan admitted in response to questions by Turnbull and by Higgins, the Opposition leader, that the Bricklin project was a high-risk venture. The Liberals pressed for details of the government's security on its investment, and Creaghan described guarantees provided by General Vehicle Inc. and Bricklin

Vehicle Corporation on the New Brunswick advances. He admitted that the two U.S. companies didn't have any "substantial assets," and that, if Bricklin Canada Ltd. went under, the assets such as body moulds and car models which were in New Brunswick might not be saleable for very much "outside this particular operation."

Creaghan, like Hatfield before him, also asserted that General Vehicle Inc., Bricklin's U.S. company, had slightly over $14 million invested in the development of the Bricklin car. It was a figure that Bricklin had provided to the government, and that government members used readily without checking. In fact, Bricklin had about $2 million invested in his car before he came to New Brunswick. The $2 million was loans from U.S. banks.

The government would release later a sketchy statement of Bricklin Canada Ltd. expenses up to May 31, 1974. The statement would show that the New Brunswick company had spent $1.2 million until that point testing car prototypes that the New Brunswick government believed Bricklin had already developed when the June, 1973 agreement was signed. The $1.2 million would be described as "an allocated portion of prototype costs related to manufacturing." The words could only have been Bricklin's. They meant that the New Brunswick company was paying the costs for the development of a production-model car at Livonia. The statement contained other curious entries, including a $303,309 expense for "special travel." A note described this expense as "travel identifiable with the plant, tooling and equipment functions of the facility establishment." The entry was an indication of the amount of money spent by Bricklin personnel, including Malcolm and Albert, on flights between Livonia. Saint John, New York and Fredericton in attempts to pull the disparate organization together. There was also an entry of $781,855 that included "an allocated portion of Detroit design expenditures and Saint John expenditures related to manufacturing engineering as opposed to basic vehicle design." This was simply another charge by Bricklin's U.S. companies to the New Brunswick company. New Brunswick, not Bricklin, was paying the costs of developing the Bricklin car. It was not what the province's officials had intended when they saw Bricklin's short film of a hand-made prototype car in 1973.

Chapter 8

WE'RE BUILDING A BETTER NEW BRUNSWICK

The Bricklin project, from beginning to end, was marked by a dichotomy reflected in Malcolm Bricklin himself. Bricklin was a car promoter and not a car manufacturer, and the Bricklin project had his unmistakeable stamp. In the summer of 1974, the dichotomy was most evident. By July, the Bricklin car was a sensation in the automotive world. Seasoned automotive writers could find only superlatives to describe it. As a promotion, the Bricklin project was unrivalled. But while the trade magazines and Bricklin were celebrating the new car, Bricklin's production personnel were working frantically to solve even the most basic processes required to put the Bricklin on the market.

The split running through the project deserves illustration. Bricklin has a talent for persuading people to part with their money. By the summer of 1974, he would have persuaded 200 U.S. car dealers to part with more than $1 million in franchise fees for a car that wasn't even in production. He would have talked them out of additional money for parts and tools and Bricklin signs that didn't exist. He would even have persuaded them to pay a dollar apiece for brochures that the rest of the industry gives away. On the strength of the brochures alone, he would have pre-sold thousands of cars. And while he was selling his car, Bricklin officials in New Brunswick were still trying to find a way to make Bricklin car bodies.

In early May, 1974, with their production schedules in a shambles, Gerald Hodgeson and Jack Hennessey approached the New Brunswick Research and Productivity Council (RPC) for advice on the problem of bonding fibreglass and acrylic to make car body parts. The council, a government agency, provides technical research and advice to industries. Members of the council suggested that the Bricklin officials investigate whether the bonding processes proposed by Van Nortwick, who was still experimenting in his office at the Minto plant, had been proven anywhere in the world. The Bricklin organization lacked the personnel to undertake such a study, so the RPC agreed to do it. The council made its first report to Hodgeson and Hennessey in mid-June, less than two weeks before Bricklin was to present his car to the world at an unveiling ceremony in New York. The RPC report said that the chemistry of bonding fibreglass to acrylic was not fully understood anywhere. Four companies, located in Texas, Tennessee, Pennsylvania and Germany, claimed to have done it, and offered their assistance.

Another ten companies claimed that, while they hadn't found a bonding formula, they could assist in the search for one.

On June 27, two days after Bricklin's jubilant New York opening, the RPC brought Professor Archie Hamielec from McMaster University in Hamilton to work on the bonding problem. Hamielec, a polymer expert, concluded that bonding could be properly obtained only when the inter-face molecules on the acrylic and fibreglass were entangled. In a July 9 report, the RPC recommended a series of tests of various mixes to determine which mix would provide the best bonding results.

To speed their work, the RPC officials asked Hodgeson for tests developed by Bricklin personnel to determine whether body parts were truly stuck. Hodgeson replied that the only test was one proposed by Albert Bricklin. Parts would be struck with a seven-pound hammer when they came off the presses. If they didn't fly apart, they were stuck. The RPC officials were curious about the background of technology that Bricklin had developed for his car. They pursued the matter with Hennessey. What did the Bricklin company own by way of engineering and manufacturing rights? Hennessey told them, according to RPC sources, that he didn't know what in Hell the Bricklins owned. In fact, the Bricklins didn't own any rights or patents. The $1 million in design and manufacturing rights that the New Brunswick government had accepted in 1973 as justification for Bricklin's 49 per cent ownership in Bricklin Canada Ltd. was simply a figure suggested by Bricklin.

The RPC staff proceeded with their tests. Bonding mixes were tried and abandoned. The RPC workers soon discovered that the acrylic was quite flammable. They also discovered that ultra-violet light (sunlight) would pass through the acrylic panels. Most polyester adhesives were susceptible to light rays — they might deteriorate under constant sunlight. Moreover, the RPC studies determined that the acrylic and fibreglass had different rates of thermal expansion. The RPC officials began to wonder if acrylic panels would change shape or even peel off in high temperature regions such as the Arizona desert.

While the RPC studies were progressing, some experimental parts began to move off the Minto assembly line. The process would continue throughout the summer as the Minto personnel struggled to get into production. On this hit-and-miss basis, which continued well into the production period, the waste would be incredible. According to Bricklin sources, 60 per cent of the acrylic used in the first months of production at Minto was lost in the parts-pressing and bonding operations. Literally truckloads of wasted acrylic and fibreglass were taken weekly to a nearby dump. Of the parts produced, another 10 per cent were lost through damage during shipment to the assembly plant at Saint John. When the parts arrived in Saint John, they had to be hand-trimmed during fitting operations. Because of the vast wastage of materials and time, the cost of components for the first car bodies produced at Minto was estimated by Bricklin officials to be in excess of $50,000 each — a far cry from the $170 per car that Albert Bricklin had demanded in January, and the $440 that Hodgeson had insisted was more realistic.

In July, with publicity building in the wake of his successful New York opening, Bricklin was under pressure to begin production. At the time of the opening, he had sold franchises to more than 200 dealers, many of whom had been waiting a year for cars. There was another factor. The April re-financing was running out. Bricklin would soon need more millions of dollars. He had to begin producing cars. He had announced at the New York opening that production would begin at Saint John within a week — an announcement that had left his production personnel shaking their heads. They had been responsible for the frantic efforts to put together the hand-produced cars for Bricklin's New York show. They knew the New Brunswick plants weren't ready to go into production. But Bricklin was worried that his credibility would slip even further if production was pushed back again. He instructed his production personnel to make preparations for a ceremony in early August to mark the beginning of the manufacture of Bricklin cars. Then Bricklin began to make his own preparations.

Bricklin's preparations were typical. He arranged for 135 journalists and Bricklin dealers to be flown by chartered jet from Philadelphia for the Saint John opening. Through Jack Hennessey, he arranged for In-Sight Productions of Toronto to cover the Bricklin opening and to produce a $10,000 film. The film, a predictably uncritical portrait of Bricklin, was later telecast across Canada on the Canadian Broadcasting Corporation network. It made Bricklin a household word in Canada.

Hennessey knew the Bricklin plants in New Brunswick weren't ready to go into production, and he was annoyed by Bricklin's pressure to stage an opening in early August. However, Hennessey also knew he wasn't in the Bricklins' good books. He had made an enemy of Albert Bricklin in February. Malcolm Bricklin had subsequently ignored Hennessey's representations for better organization on the project. Hennessey could perceive that his position in the organization was weakening. At the same time, he was becoming more frustrated with the unending production problems. He knew he couldn't object to Bricklin's production plans without jeopardizing his position even further. So he contented himself with telling Bricklin to remember to invite some New Brunswick dignitaries to the August opening, to complement the 135-member crew he was flying in from Philadelphia. Bricklin took the suggestion petulantly, according to Hennessey. Hennessey realized he wouldn't be with Bricklin much longer.

On Tuesday, August 6, Bricklin's entourage and a large crowd of local people gathered outside the Bricklin plant in Saint John's Grandview industrial park for ceremonies to mark the beginning of production. There was a round of speech-making. Albert Bricklin spoke of Malcolm's years of faith in the Bricklin car. Malcolm had been able to spread this faith to bankers, the New Brunswick government, car dealers, and production officials from other car-manufacturing companies, said Albert. Premier Hatfield described the car as the most sophisticated product ever made in New Brunswick. "We're not just building a car. We're building a better New Brunswick," he said. Hatfield also said he believed the Bricklin would become "a symbol of what New Brunswick and its people can do." After the speeches, Hatfield and Malcolm Bricklin walked into the plant. There was a sound of an engine starting. The first Bricklin emerged from the plant with Hatfield in the passenger's seat and Malcolm behind the wheel. One of the headlights was closed in a frozen wink. The crowd cheered. No other cars came out of the plant. Bricklin wasn't ready to go into production. The first car to come off the assembly line was, like the New York models, a hand-built car. It was used later in crash tests. A week after the Saint John ceremony, Bricklin's production would remain at one car. Minto was still attempting to solve the car body problems. At a press conference after the Saint John ceremony, Bricklin announced that his car would sell for $7,490 — it was the third price increase he had announced in a year.

After the ceremonies, Jack Hennessey approached Bricklin. Hennessey wanted to talk. He wanted to clear up questions about his own position in the Bricklin organization. He wanted to know how much authority he still had. Was he still the vice-president and general manager of the New Brunswick plants?

"Morie (Adams) is," Bricklin said.

The next day, Hennessey wrote his letter of resignation and sent it to Bricklin. Bricklin said they would have to get together again and talk things over. Bricklin had to catch a plane. It was the last Hennessey ever saw of him.

The same week, Albert Bricklin fired Gerald Hodgeson, who, like Hennessey, had been critical of the Bricklins throughout the frustrating months of non-production. "It was due to a very severe difference over operation methods," Hodgeson told a reporter. He described himself as "very much a critic," and said the Bricklins considered him a disruptive influence. Later, Hodgeson would describe the Bricklins as being "full of vim and vigor and nothing else." Hennessey said only that his departure was "purely personal, it had nothing to do with the future or potential" of the Bricklin car.

In late August, Vic Scully, Rose's protege, replaced the fired Hodgeson as manager of the Minto plant. Scully had been working under Hodgeson, supervising plant technicians who were working on the bonding problems and on the installation of presses and tooling. The Bricklins instructed Scully to dismiss RPC from further work on the bonding problems. Bricklin technicians would continue the work. The technicians, several of whom were on loan from ETM, one of the companies that had provided temporary tooling, would make improvements in the bonding processes in the remaining months of 1974. The small presses would be adapted to the acrylic, largely through the work of Jerry Lienert, who had been transferred to Minto from his position as engineering manager at the Saint John plant. But throughout the production period, there would continue to be problems with bonding and there would be a constant high rate of materials loss through scrap. In 1975, the scrap loss would still be running at 15 per cent to 25 per cent.

After the Saint John opening, with the New Brunswick plants still struggling to solve production problems, Bricklin and Jonas Halperin, an official with the publicity firm of Rogers and Cowan, went skilfully to work to build publicity for the Bricklin car. The publicity was needed. Many of Bricklin's 200 dealers were beginning to doubt that the Bricklin car existed. To stave them off, Bricklin would fly groups of dealers to Saint John in coming months to prove that cars were being produced. A group of 147 dealers and journalists would be flown, free of charge, by chartered jet from New York on September 10. Another group of eighty-four would be flown from Boston. They would watch as many as two cars an hour come off the assembly line in the fall of 1974. The publicity created by Halperin and Bricklin was needed for another reason. Bricklin knew that his major selling point with the New Brunswick government was the marketability of the Bricklin car. In coming months, the government would defend new outlays of money to Bricklin on grounds that there was a ready market for the car, and that only production problems were preventing Bricklin from making money.

Throughout August, the Bricklin car was the talk of the automotive magazines. Many of the articles stemmed from the Saint John opening, to which Halperin had invited a number of influential magazine writers. But the articles weren't restricted to the trade magazines. Halperin is one of the most influential and well-connected

U.S. publicity agents. With a lifetime in public relations, and extensive experience in the promotion of movie stars, he had ins to nearly every major talk show and magazine in the U.S., including the sex and glamor magazines. Halperin persuaded *Playboy* magazine to feature the Bricklin car in its September, 1974 issue — an issue that sold out on New Brunswick newstands within two days, and was soon going locally for $10 second hand. The Bricklin car was even featured in a movie version of the Harold Robbins novel, *The Betsy*.

An indication of the intensity of the promotion is contained in a release that the New Brunswick Information Service, the government's publicity agency, was instructed to issue in the late summer of 1974. The release, which was telexed to newsrooms throughout New Brunswick, quoted "some of the samples of comment which are gaining the (Bricklin) automobile and the province national and continent-wide attention." The release contained sample quotes from nearly a dozen well-known magazines. "The Bricklin," said a quote from *Playboy* magazine, which had put a Bricklin car and playgirls together in its September issue, "has a gutsy, don't-tread-on-me look about it — somewhere between a Datsun 240Z and a Maserati Ghibli, with Mercedes 300 SL-like gull wings thrown in for good measure . . . plus a raft of safety features." *Coronet* magazine described the Bricklin car as "long, sleek and classy," resembling "the most expensive European car." *Coronet* also asserted that "Malcolm Bricklin's investment gamble is a pretty safe bet." *Saga* magazine was equally uncritical. "It's not just another car," said *Saga*, "It's the vehicle that may revolutionize the automotive industry."

The publicity was far from accurate. Despite the claims of success, the Bricklin project was on the verge of bankruptcy in the fall of 1974. Even after production began, it would remain close to collapse, held together only by vast new amounts of money from New Brunswick. Despite the magazine articles, the Bricklin car was not even completely engineered in the fall of 1974. It would go into production without complete specifications. Once in production, the losses would be astonishing. Bricklin, partly because of incompetent management, could not produce cars at a profit.

A confidential computer printout prepared in late 1974 would list 968 parts for the Bricklin car, but even this list of specifications would be incomplete. Many of the parts would change as Bricklin changed suppliers, often, according to company sources, because the suppliers put him on a cash basis after being paid with rubber cheques. The computer printout would list chassis, body and drive train costs at $4,093 per car, but many of the parts listed on the printout were not even priced. Because of the erratic, constantly-changing parts supply,

Bricklin production personnel could not obtain reliable cost projections for many parts. As the Bricklin plants struggled towards production in the late summer of 1974, the parts costs would soar beyond control. According to Bricklin sources, the parts costs would remain at more than $7,200 per car for much of the production period, excluding body parts wastage at Minto and Saint John, which was running as high as 25 per cent. Bricklin had only a handful of parts supply contracts, although he was supposed to have obtained all major supply contracts in 1973, according to the terms of the financing provided by the New Brunswick government in its June, 1973, agreement. In late 1974, Bricklin was buying parts wherever he could find them, often at retail prices and always in small quantities, in an effort to get into production. To receive an assured supply of parts at wholesale prices, he would have had to pre-order, giving suppliers the lead-time required to obtain or produce the parts. Bricklin had not had the money to pre-order. The money provided by New Brunswick in 1973 and the first half of 1974 was not used for operating capital, as was intended. It was used largely to engineer the Bricklin car.

The haphazard parts supply system, which lasted throughout the production period, would contribute to high labor costs for the Bricklin car. Workers would be pulled from the assembly line to finish incomplete cars as parts arrived. Often the workers would simply stand around with nothing to do. There were no parts for them to install. In their anxiety to keep the assembly line moving, certain Bricklin officials, such as Ian Watson, the Bricklin Canada Ltd. comptroller, would often spend evenings lounging in the Saint John airport, hoping that a late flight would bring parts, often bought at retail prices, that were needed for production the next day. In these circumstances, labor costs were enormous. Productivity was dismal. According to Bricklin sources, the cost of labor averaged over $6,300 for each Bricklin car. According to the same sources, the cost in parts and labor at Saint John and Minto for the first 800 cars was at least $16,000 each. This figure doesn't include such overhead costs as plant rent and bank interest. After the first 800 cars, production costs were pulled down gradually to about $13,500 per car. Despite the high costs, Bricklin Canada Ltd. charged Bricklin's U.S. companies $5,400 for each car, resulting in a loss to the New Brunswick company of more than $11,000 on each of the first 800 cars produced. In April, 1975, at the government's insistence, the transfer price would be increased to $7,200. By that time, production costs would be reduced to about $13,500. The loss to the New Brunswick company was still about $6,000 per car.

Chapter 9

THE BY-ELECTIONS

In the late summer of 1974, Hatfield was planning his government's re-election strategy. There was frequent speculation in the press about an autumn election. Throughout the summer, Hatfield had prepared the groundwork, carefully picking issues designed to throw the Opposition Liberals on the defensive. He had announced that his government would finance the construction of a nuclear plant near Saint John, in the home territory of the Opposition leader, Robert Higgins. To reassure his English supporters while asserting the equal language rights of the province's Acadian minority, he had attacked a decision by the neighboring province of Quebec to make French its only official language. But Hatfield had another worrisome issue to contend with. What role should the Bricklin car play in his election strategy?

Hatfield suspected that the Opposition Liberals would carry out a whispering campaign against his government's financing of Bricklin. But he knew they wouldn't openly condemn the financing because the Bricklin project, which was finally in production, was creating jobs in Saint John and Minto. Characteristically, Hatfield decided to take the offensive and make the Bricklin car a central issue, thus exploiting the Liberals' hesitancy. He would, as he had at the Saint John opening, portray the Bricklin as a symbol of New Brunswick's progress, and he would cast the Liberals in the role of doubters and skeptics who were harming New Brunswick. Hatfield's decision had two consequences. First, it linked his government's fortunes firmly to those of the Bricklin car. Secondly, it left the government completely vulnerable to requests by Bricklin officials for more money. By the fall of 1974, Bricklin had exhausted the three-way financing provided in April and he needed money again. Bricklin couldn't attract outside investors because he had no security to offer — his security was tied up in the earlier investments. The only conceivable source of funds was the New Brunswick government. Joseph Rose, Bricklin's financial advisor, readily admitted in a later interview that Bricklin officials realized an election was a good time to raise money from the government. Throughout the 1974 election campaign and its immediate aftermath, Bricklin officials wore a path to the government's door with requests for funds, and the government complied. In the middle of an election campaign, the government couldn't afford to let the project go under.

With his stategy set, Hatfield surveyed his election prospects. There were two long-standing vacancies in the provincial legislature. One was in rural York County, outside Fredericton, traditionally a Conservative preserve. The other was in the urban riding of Campbellton in northern New Brunswick. It had been a swing riding in earlier elections. Hatfield decided to test the waters by calling by-elections to fill the two vacancies. The by-elections were called for September 30. Depending on their outcome, he would have ample time to call a fall general election.

Hatfield quickly injected the Bricklin issue into the by-election campaigns. At a convention to choose a Conservative candidate for the York County by-election, he raised the issues of the nuclear plant and the Quebec government's language legislation, and then moved resolutely on to the Bricklin. It was plainly what the assembled Conservatives wanted to hear. Many of them had watched with misgiving as the government's investment in the car company rose, and now, sweltering in their shirtsleeves at the late-August convention, they were glad to hear a defence. Hatfield told them the Bricklin project had overcome many obstacles on its way to production, but the worst one it faced was the provincial Liberals who were "the foremost spokesmen in Canada on what was wrong with the enterprise." He accused the Liberals of having done "all they could to undermine public confidence, to run down its (Bricklin's) prospects all over Canada and to damage its image in the eyes of millions." The Liberals had so little faith in the province that they didn't believe it could make cars. "It couldn't be done in New Brunswick because we are not supposed to be doing things like that here," he said. "Well, I believe we are going to prove them wrong, and that it will be a great thing for this province."

Faced with Hatfield's attacks, the Liberals were uncertain how to react. John Turnbull, the Opposition's Bricklin critic, made an appearance at a Liberal nominating convention in York County a week later and criticized the project, but Higgins, the Liberal leader, declined to take up Hatfield's challenge. The Liberal by-election candidates resorted to local issues in the campaigns.

After taking his initial step in York County, Hatfield plunged. He drove a bright orange Bricklin to Campbellton where he campaigned on behalf of Fernand Dube, the Conservative candidate. The Bricklin was owned by Bricklin Canada Ltd., and had been designated a public relations car. In Campbellton, it was a sensation. Hatfield drove the car to a lodge-opening ceremony at Sugarloaf Park, outside Campbellton, and the crowd quickly forgot the ceremonies and rushed to inspect the new car. Hatfield and Dube shook hands with the gathering crowd. The only detractor was a candidate for the little-supported New Democratic

Party, who took advantage of the occasion to hand out party stickers and to pronounce that the car would be the biggest flop since the government-financed Westmorland Chemical Park went under in the mid-sixties. Maruice Harquail, the Liberal candidate, attempted later to separate the Bricklin issue from his own campaign. "The Bricklin has nothing whatsoever to do with this riding," he said. "I cannot see the connection to Campbellton when all the jobs are being given to the south." But in spite of Harquail's protests, the Bricklin car was bowling over the Campbellton voters.

On September 30, the two ridings voted. The Conservative candidates walked away with the by-elections. Their Liberal opponents were left far behind, with tire tracks up their backs. Less than two weeks later, Hatfield announced a November 18 general election. It was to become the Bricklin election. No other name would do.

On October 4, four days after the by-election votes, R.A. Woods Co. Ltd., a Saint John construction firm, placed a $29,294 mechanic's lien against the Bricklin plant in Saint John for non-payment of bills on renovations done by the construction firm at the plant. Like many of Bricklin's other bills, they were months overdue. Bricklin would ignore the lien until early November, when, with the general election campaign under way, a reporter discovered it. Then the bills would be paid. The lien would contribute to a government decision during the campaign to buy the plant, which was owned by T.S. Simms and Co. Ltd., and rent it to Bricklin.

On October 8, Economic Growth Minister Paul Creaghan announced that the New Brunswick government would make a $2 million "shareholder's loan" to Bricklin to provide the company with operating capital. It was the first of several loans the government would make to Bricklin during the election period. It was the only one to be made public before the campaign was over. Three days after Creaghan's announcement, Hatfield made his announcement of a November 18 election. In response to a reporter's questions, he said the $2 million loan announced by Creaghan was not intended to keep Bricklin afloat during an election campaign.

On November 2, while provincial politicians were beating the cold New Brunswick hustings for votes, Bricklin was glorying in a spectacular promotion at his Phoenix raceway, the testing-ground for Bricklin cars. The promotion was the first Arizona 150, a car race that featured such motoring greats as Bobby Unser, Mario Andretti, Johnny Rutherford and Gordon Johncock. The ceremonies included Senator Barry Goldwater, a former Republican presidential candidate, who led a parade around the track, and five New Brunswick-built Bricklins, one of which was driven by Malcolm. The Bricklins were piped around the track by a United States air force band. Onlookers included Arizona Governor Jack Williams and Prince Faisal of Saudi Arabia.

Much later, in February, 1975, the government would release a sparse statement of Bricklin Canada Ltd.'s expenses to October 31, 1974. The statement would give some indication of Bricklin's financial position at the beginning of the election campaign. It would show that Bricklin had spent $15.4 million from June, 1973 to October 31, 1974. Excluding inventories of $3.15 million, the company had spent $12.2 million. In the same period, the company had built only about 100 cars. None of the cars were saleable. All of them were missing parts. They were shipped to Bricklin dealers as showroom models. In October, 1974, Bricklin would have been bankrupt without more New Brunswick money. In the last three months of 1974, Bricklin would get about $7 million more. Even that wouldn't be enough.

Chapter 10

THE BRICKLIN ELECTION

On November 7, 1974, an orange car with gull-wing doors drove into Sackville, a sleepy university town in southeastern New Brunswick. A crowd gathered because the Bricklin car had not been seen in Sackville before. A gull-wing door opened and the premier of New Brunswick emerged. "You are probably wondering if I am trying to sell a car or if I am trying to get elected," Hatfield said.

The Opposition Liberals were uncertain of what to do with the Bricklin issue in the campaign. They were afraid of openly attacking the project because it was creating jobs. At the same time, they realized that Hatfield would make the Bricklin a central issue, as he had done in the September by-elections. The Liberals, who tended in the 1974 campaign to accent the personal qualities of Higgins, their leader, and to treat issues as if they were dodge-balls, were in a quandary. To cover themselves, they attempted to beat a path up the middle. With Higgins' approval, John Turnbull announced the Liberals' position on Bricklin at an October 25 nominating convention in Saint John. Turnbull called for a feasibility study and a financial audit of Bricklin Canada Ltd. and its associated companies. He also said that competent businessmen should be consulted before a decision was made "as to the extent of future financial support." Thus committed, the Liberals proceeded to launch a whispering campaign against the project outside Saint John, ridiculing it freely whenever the provincial media wasn't present.

Sensing the Liberal vacuum, and hoping to cut off the whispering campaign, Hatfield drove the orange Bricklin extensively in the campaign. And while he drove, his government made new financial commitments to keep Bricklin out of bankruptcy. The commitments were not disclosed until after the election.

The first commitment was made on November 6. Five days earlier, the government had received notice that Bricklin Canada Ltd. had been placed under threat of eviction from its rented plant in Saint John because it couldn't meet the terms of its lease. Bricklin had agreed to purchase the plant from T.S. Simms and Co. Ltd. by July 31, 1974, but the lease was extended until October 31 because Bricklin couldn't afford to buy the plant in July. In letters dated October 30 and 31, the Simms company informed the government that Bricklin would be evicted if the plant wasn't purchased. Simms suggested that the government buy the plant. "Presently, we feel that Simms is being placed in the unfair position of helping to finance Bricklin," T.S. Simms, company president, said in an October 30 letter to the economic growth department. "It is well known that we have fully co-operated with Bricklin during the last sixteen months — even to the extent of releasing Bricklin from any legal action in respect to non-completion of the sale agreement last July . . . Under the strain of its current financial obligations, Simms cannot afford to continue to hinge its fate on the destiny of the Bricklin venture." The letter also noted that a mechanic's lien had been placed against the plant because of Bricklin debts. On November 6, less than a week after it received the letters, the government decided to buy the Simms' plant for $1.54 million and lease it to Bricklin.

On November 6, the same day that the decision was made to purchase the Saint John plant, Hatfield traveled to Campbellton to campaign. An attack of viral laryngitis had silenced him in the preceding half-week (cabinet ministers had accompanied him to rallies to read his speeches, and Hatfield had exchanged wordless handshakes with voters — he quipped later that Higgins had been equally silent), but on November 6, he recovered his voice. In response to questions at a Campbellton meeting, he defended the Bricklin project. Bricklin had no more severe problems than any other plant at its outset, he insisted. "There are always problems in the beginning," he went on. "Bricklin's main problem at the moment is getting parts. There is nothing technically wrong. There is a market for more Bricklin cars than can be produced in Saint John, and the future of the operation looks very bright indeed."

Although he had appeared in a Bricklin during the Campbellton by-election campaign, Hatfield had left the orange car (which local wags quickly dubbed The Great Pumpkin) outside the Lord Beaverbrook Hotel in Fredericton in the early stages of the provincial campaign. But on November 7, he drove the car into Sackville, where it was a sensation. From then until voting day, the orange Bricklin would travel New Brunswick, a visible symbol of Hatfield's campaign. "In Sackville," Jacqueline Webster reported in the Fredericton *Daily Gleaner* on November 8, "groups of people gathered within minutes each time he (Hatfield) made a stop, and at Mount Allison University enough students were on hand to fill an average classroom. No sooner was he out of the car than someone else was inside, underneath or around it." Hatfield, Webster reported, was "obviously pleased" with the attention the car attracted. "I am proud of the Bricklin," he told one group in Sackville, "because it is a symbol of what can be accomplished in this province and what is being accomplished."

Later in the day, Hatfield disclosed the terms of the $2 million October shareholder's loan to Bricklin, which had not been made public at the time of the loan. Among the terms was a provision for royalty payments to the province on Bricklin cars shipped to the U.S. The province would receive $25 per car for the first 40,000 cars shipped, and $50 per car for the next 180,000. The province would also have an option to purchase 200,000 General Vehicle shares at one cent apiece. The province would receive a personal guarantee from Malcolm Bricklin for repayment of the $2 million loan — the first personal guarantee the province had requested in its financing of Bricklin. "That car is going to sell," Hatfield said, after disclosing the loan terms. "Bricklin is assured of an excellent market. Already it has orders for forty thousand cars and the arrangement announced today enables the province to share fully in its success." However, he declined to mention that Bricklin had already pledged royalties to the First Pennsylvania Bank, along with personal guarantees. He also declined to mention that total Bricklin production from August, when production began, until November 7 was 180 complete cars — far below the 1,000 cars a month that Bricklin said in September would be coming off the line by October. The province subsequently would defer its right to royalty payments until such time as Bricklin was making a profit. Bricklin never made a profit. The royalties were, to say the least, dubious security for a $2 million loan.

Even while Hatfield was announcing the terms of the October 2 loan, his government was considering a new request from Bricklin for more money. Unable to raise production, Bricklin was sinking further behind with his creditors. On November 8, the day after Hatfield announced the October loan terms, the Conservative cabinet approved a new loan of $1 million to Bricklin for operating capital. The loan was not revealed until after the election. Under its terms, the province would receive a further royalty of $6.25 per car on the first 40,000 cars shipped by Bricklin, and a further $12.50 per car on the next 180,000 shipped. In addition, the province would increase its share ownership in Bricklin Canada Ltd. from 51 per cent, which it had held since the company was formed, to 67 per cent. It would also receive options on a further 200,000 shares in General Vehicle at one cent apiece. The new royalties were of equally dubious value as security. At this point, the government was simply bankrolling the Bricklin companies to keep them from collapse.

On November 9, the beginning of the Remembrance Day weekend, Hatfield was on the road again with his orange Bricklin. Over the weekend, he campaigned in the cluster of northwestern ridings that make up Madawaska County, a swing area. In the final week of the campaign, he resorted more frequently to a helicopter to get him into the province's diverse ridings, but the Bricklin still put in appearances. On November 14, Hatfield drove the car to a student 'under attack' session at the University of New Brunswick in Fredericton, where it attracted a crowd. During the attack session, Hatfield said he didn't believe the books of Bricklin Canada Ltd. should be made public because the company was a private one, even though the province owned a majority of its shares. The students also raised questions about a recent *Financial Post* article containing allegations of widespread political patronage in New Brunswick. Hatfield said in response to the questions that he believed patronage would always be a fact of life in the province. It was a statement with which the Liberals could have gone to town, but they declined to pick it up. The Liberals were accenting Higgins and motherhood.

On November 18, the province voted. Hatfield drove with his mother in a white Bricklin to a polling station in the small town of Hartland on the St. John River, and cast a ballot. He had grown up in Hartland, and had represented the potato-belt area in the provincial legislature since 1961, when he was wet-eared and twenty-nine.

With the returns indicating the re-election of his government, Hatfield went to the Lord Beaverbrook Hotel in Fredericton for a celebration organized by the Conservatives. Party supporters swelled the lobby of the old hotel. Among them was Malcolm Bricklin, who had an interest in the election. More than an interest, in fact. His very livelihood depended on it. The Liberals would likely have shut him down, if elected. After accepting congratulations, Hatfield held a short press conference. He was happy with the support the Conservatives had drawn in traditionally Liberal areas of the province, particularly the French-speaking areas. The Conservatives had picked up four seats in the north, breaking a decades-old Liberal hegemony. But Hatfield said he was disappointed by Liberal gains in the cities of Moncton and Saint John. He declined to speculate on whether the Conservative losses in Saint John, where the Liberals took four of six seats and narrowly lost another, had anything to do with the Bricklin car. However, he said it appeared that Saint John didn't accept his government's development policies.

The next day, Hatfield left for a week-long vacation. The election had given his Conservatives 33 seats and the Liberals 25.

On November 20, two days after the election, the Fredericton CBC radion station (CBZ) recorded an interview with Malcolm Bricklin. Bricklin admitted he was having production problems. Less than 300 cars had been shipped from the plant in Saint John. Parts shortages, car quality problems and low productivity were hurting. (In an effort to overcome some of these problems, Bricklin had begun a

'Pride and Quality Team' program in October. The prize for high quality work would be the posting on a bulletin board of a life-size photograph of the leader of the winning team). But Bricklin still expected to be producing 20 to 25 cars a day in December, and 50 a day by February or March. There was no problem with demand. Bricklin dealers in the U.S. had taken deposits from buyers for four years' production of cars. Would he be needing any more money from the province? "Absolutely," Bricklin said. "It's no surprise. It's all part of our continuing projections, that we've been, you know, supplying to the province and to our banks on a continuing basis." How much money did he need? Oh, he thought, six to eight million. When? "We'll be back, I am sure," said Bricklin, "in the next week or two, talking to them about projections that they have received many months ago."

Bricklin's bombshell caused consternation even among government members. Pressed for a reaction, Economic Growth Minister Paul Creaghan insisted that he was "not surprised" Bricklin needed more money, but he said the government would have to look carefully at the request "to give it the kind of consideration that is based on business principles and what's in the best interest of the province as a whole."

A week later, Hatfield told a reporter, "The government will probably have to put more money into the project unless it can be found from private sources. The government is in this kind of position where it apparently is the only source that will take a risk. We have confidence in the future, unlike the banks and unlike some governments." Hatfield still had not forgiven the federal government for its lack of early support for Bricklin.

Chapter 11

THE GROWING CONTROVERSY

Bricklin's revelations of his money needs, followed by disclosures that the government had funded Bricklin during the election campaign, stirred New Brunswick's newspapers to a degree unusual since the mid-sixties when the newspapers had battled daily, and sometimes viciously, over the Equal Opportunities reforms of Premier Louis Robichaud's Liberal government. In the aftermath of the reforms, which abolished New Brunswick's old regime of county councils and transferred all but local services to the province, a mood of reconciliation had settled in. Politicians were polite to one another again. With few exceptions, the province's newspapers drifted into a middle-of-the-road position, content to avoid as many toes as possible. When editorial writers felt inclined to let down their hair, they attacked drunken drivers and anti-monarchists. The Bricklin election changed that. In its aftermath, the government ran into concerted newspaper criticism over Bricklin. The criticism was led by the Saint John *Telegraph-Journal* which, on occasion, flayed Hatfield almost daily in its editorial pages.

On November 22, two days after Bricklin said he needed more money, the *Telegraph-Journal* went on the streets with an editorial entitled: 'How much more?' "On Monday of this week, election day in New Brunswick," it began, "Premier Richard Hatfield was highly visible as he tooled around his home constituency in a nifty little Bricklin, selling himself and the New Brunswick-built car in which the province has invested so much interest and money." In the closing stages of the campaign, the editorial noted, Hatfield had also appeared in television promotions with the Bricklin car, and had talked about the industries his government was creating. "He also continued to remind voters that Richard Hatfield was a man of his word, that he was a man who made and kept promises, that his word was good." What, then, to make of Bricklin's announcement that he needed $6-million to $8-million? "Did Premier Hatfield know that millions more dollars were needed last week, while he was driving the Bricklin car around New Brunswick as part of his election campaign? And if he didn't know, why didn't he?" The editorial said that Hatfield had put "so much unusual emphasis" on the car that it became a symbol of his election campaign. "The premier has some explaining to do," the editorial concluded, "and he'd better get on with it promptly. Because he is the one who promoted the Bricklin and he is the one who went on television to tell New Brunswickers about his integrity and his good word." The following day, *The Daily Gleaner* in Fredericton cited the dangers of "throwing good money after bad," and concluded that "the Bricklin business" had cast a shadow over the beginning of Hatfield's second term.

On November 28, Hatfield, who had just returned from a week-long vacation, said in an interview in Toronto that his government was prepared to put more money into Bricklin. He described the car project as a "good investment" because of market demand for the Bricklin, and added that he had said during the election campaign he would be prepared to invest further.

Opposition politicians jumped on his statements. "It's just a fraud," howled John Turnbull, who had won re-election in the riding of Saint John Harbour. "He (Hatfield) never mentioned it during the election campaign. It's just as simple as that." Albert Richardson, leader of the provincial New Democratic Party which won three per cent of the popular vote and no seats in the election, accused Hatfield of "bungling and misleading the people of New Brunswick," and called for an inquiry.

With criticism mounting, Bricklin instructed Morie Adams, the manager of his New Brunswick operations, to issue a statement to the effect that Bricklin was overcoming its production problems, and soon would be raising production levels. The Saint John plant would move to two shifts in January, said Adams. It was producing two cars an hour and would move to three cars an hour by early December. The plant had produced 302 cars since it went into operation in August. Shortly after Adams' statement, Hatfield's office issued a statement that the government was looking for a consultant to study "the viability" of the Bricklin project. (The search for a consultant would take some time because consultants are a rarity in the automotive industry. It is an industry practice to require what amount to five-year vows of silence from retiring executives, in order to protect trade secrets. The New Brunswick government eventually would select Wespac Planning Consultants Ltd. of British Columbia, on the recommendation of Nason, the deputy economic growth minister. Nason would say in a later interview that Wespac was suggested to him by Sandy Peel, his counterpart in B.C. Clifford Sawyer, a Wespac consultant who would be assigned to the Bricklin project, was a Conservative party worker in B.C. Sawyer was also a former Ford executive).

With reporters flooding his office with calls, Hatfield called a press conference in Fredericton on December 2. Economic Growth Minister Paul Creaghan also attended, and several members of the Conservative caucus, who had been conferring with Hatfield over the formation of his new cabinet, drifted into seats in the back of the conference room to watch. Sipping frequently from a glass of water (he had given up smoking during the election campaign), Hatfield read a lengthy introductory statement in which he reviewed his government's financing of Bricklin — revealing for the first time the government's $1 million loan to Bricklin on November 8, and its decision to buy the Saint John plant that Bricklin had been leasing. His statement made no mention of the threat by T.S. Simms and Co. Ltd. to evict Bricklin if the plant wasn't purchased. In an attempt to dispel accusations that his government had misled voters by not revealing the election financing of Bricklin, Hatfield took pains to describe what he called the "normal" procedure for disclosing investments. "On the recommendation of the minister of economic growth," he said, "funds are authorized by cabinet to Provincial Holdings Ltd., the Crown agency through which the government invests (in fact, takes equity positions) in certain industries . . . The particular industry for which the money is advanced is not immediately made public. This is because Provincial Holdings, whose directors are the ministers of economic growth, finance and treasury board as well as several senior civil servants, still must negotiate the terms of financing; and because the government was aware that the company (Bricklin) was seeking additional sources of financing and it is not normally our policy at that stage to make known the government's decision to make additional funds available." Of course, Bricklin was seeking additional sources of financing from the moment he set foot in New Brunswick. He had been unable to honor his June, 1973, commitment to raise $1 million privately. By December, 1974 there simply were no additional sources of funds.

Hatfield also took pains to say that his government had not received a formal request from Bricklin for $6 million to $8 million. However, the government had received a request on November 29, three days before the press conference, for $2.5 million, and was still considering it. Hatfield gave every indication the request would be approved. "The government cannot leave the economic development of New Brunswick to the mercies of the Canadian banks, the Toronto boardrooms or the federal bureaucracy," he said. "Without the involvement of the provincial government, there will be no sustained economic development in New Brunswick except for the tasks these remote institutions think us capable of and suitable for." It was a theme he had used consistently since the initial investment to Bricklin was made in 1973.

When he had completed his statement, Hatfield turned to the reporters for questions. The questions came quickly.

Press: "Was it simply coincidence that the statement (Bricklin's statement that he needed $6 million to $8 million) was made two days after the election?"

Hatfield: "I . . . I . . . It was certainly coincidence that he was here after the election, yes. I had no knowledge of the statement being made or anything. I wasn't here on November 20."

Press: "And you mentioned as well, the procedure in the Royal Gazette for advertising orders-in-council, it was then, just a coincidence as well that didn't become public knowledge prior to the election, the government didn't offer that information?"

Hatfield: "The government is following the policy that it has always followed in these cases. There is nothing inconsistent or unusual about this."

Hatfield was then asked to recall when, during the election campaign, he had said that he was prepared to put more money into Bricklin.

Hatfield: "I was, I was asked a number of times during the campaign, by a number of people and I believe in interviews that I held, with a number of people, about the Bricklin project. And I am convinced that during that time I did not say . . . nor did I make a formal speech in which I said that . . . Nor did I say that. The implication of the question put to me as I remember in Toronto was that I had deliberately withheld this information. And I said that is not the case. I did mention it during the campaign."

The questions began to centre around the appointment of a consultant to Bricklin, which Hatfield's office had announced the preceding week. Lowell Murray, Hatfield's deputy minister, had said in an interview the consultant would be appointed to study "the viability" of the Bricklin project.

Hatfield: "Well, let me make it clear, that the government is not employing a consultant to test or assess or judge its decision to invest in this project. But the government is, as it has with other industries, seeking to find . . . experts, if you will, who, who will be able to assist the company in solving some of the problems that it may have in meeting its production schedule and faster in getting to a production level, which will be . . . which will return a profit to the company. But I want to make it very clear that we are not, we do not have, we do not . . . we are not opening up for questioning the viability of this project. We believe this project is definitely viable."

Hatfield's response created some confusion. The earlier statement from his office had given the impression that a consultant was being hired to determine the viability of the project, in the light of new requests by Bricklin for more money.

Press: "You wouldn't know if you will advance more money before you receive the report of the consultants?"

Hatfield: "I think, I don't . . . you're confusing that, somehow or other we're going to get a consultant's report, which is going to tell us whether or not we should advance money. That is not the policy or the plan."

Press: "The answer is yes, you could advance, regardless?"

Hatfield: "We could. We could. Yes. But you see, where the, there is no consultant's report as you phrase it, coming."

Press: "Now, in your best estimate, how long do you think the government is going to have to provide finances for the Bricklin company?"

Hatfield: "I . . . I again can't really answer that. But I do say this, the evidence is still pretty strong that it is a viable project and it is strong in the market place . . . I think that however the indications with various dealers as to the kind of demand that they have received might add up to some ways to, ah to ah, what would four years be . . . forty-eight thousand cars."

Press: "Mr. Premier, could I ask for clarity on . . . no report per se coming from any consultant so-called, that the government is satisfied with viability, and you might loan money without it, is that correct?"

Hatfield: "Yes. Let me explain. That if we expect this industry to succeed and if we expect the normal kind of operation the government can't suddenly throw a great cloud of, of doubt over it. I want to make it clear that the government has genuinely and honestly, has confidence in this project. There is again, if it could, if it could only be understood in the context of other . . . I think of a pulp and paper industry which lost $27 million before it started to make a profit. The world's full of those. We are producing a car, two cars an hour, hopefully three cars an hour. They are going out and they are being bought."

Press: "This fellow that is going to be hired, he is not necessarily going to be a consultant. What is he going to be?"

(laughter)

Hatfield: "He is going to investigate, look into, assess, the various operations of Bricklin . . . in Minto, Saint John and at the time . . . the design centre in Detroit, and see if he cannot make recommendations to the company which the government will be privileged to, to speed up production."

Hatfield had hoped to calm the growing controversy over Bricklin with his press conference, but the conference only fueled it. Political and press reaction to the press conference was furious.

"Everything, Premier Hatfield implied, was carried out in a very routine fashion," the *Telegraph-Journal* said in a lengthy editorial on

December 3, the day after the press conference. "Yes, the province had agreed to pump an extra million dollars into the Bricklin auto operation on the eve of the election. (In fact, the province had put $2 million into it — Hatfield didn't disclose at the press conference that an additional $1 million had been approved for the purchase of the Simms plant; he said only that the government intended to purchase it). No, this had not been announced publicly at that time, because this was not the way things were done.

"Yes," the editorial continued, "$500,000 had been made available on Nov. 15, and another $500,000 on Nov. 29. Yes, he was aware that Malcolm Bricklin had said in an interview that another $6,000,000 to $8,000,000 would be needed immediately. But the auto entrepreneur hadn't asked the province for that amount. He has asked the province for only $2,500,000. The province is mulling that one over.

"No, the premier said, he hadn't actually made a "formal" announcement that Bricklin would be needing millions more during the election campaign, as he had suggested in a Toronto interview last week. But he was convinced he had been making the situation known during the campaign, and did he have to say it right out?"

The editorial went on to recount Hatfield's arguments that the request for new financing was not surprising, in view of production problems at the New Brunswick plants. "So in these circumstances, why wouldn't a company need more money? It all becomes clear, the way the premier explains it, so much so that one begins to wonder why anyone would have the audacity to question the venture in the first place.

"After all, Malcolm Bricklin, the president of the company, has acknowledged that he has faced every problem imaginable, and, in candor which may endear him to the premier, but certainly not the taxpayers, he has said his projections are 'lousy.' In other words, how would a guy who makes 'lousy' projections know in the beginning when he was going to need an extra two, three, six or eight million dollars? Not to worry. He'd just ask for more when the pot started to run dry. And that's what he's been doing."

The editorial concluded that Hatfield was in an "unenviable" position. "The next fork in the road is obviously a most difficult one for the premier and it is possible to feel sorry for the man and for the lonely decision he must make — but, then, from the very beginning and by choice, he's been in the driver's seat."

The Opposition Liberals, who had just received copies of the November orders-in-council and were aware that $2 million had been committed to Bricklin during the campaign, were furious. "How can anyone, including the premier of New Brunswick and Paul Creaghan, say that the people were not misled in the election campaign . .?" demanded Higgins. "How can any reasonable and responsible person refuse to have an independent public audit and feasibility study at this time?"

With the controversy swirling, Hatfield announced the appointments to his new cabinet on December 3. The cabinet bore the stamp of earlier Hatfield cabinets — utterly loyal men who tended to go mute whenever the public light became a little harsh (Hatfield had learned a lesson in 1972 when he was forced to dismiss Charlie Van Horne, a flamboyant tourism minister and former leadership rival. Van Horne was later convicted of influence-peddling. Typically, Hatfield replaced him in 1972 with the granite-faced Jean-Paul LeBlanc). Creaghan, much to his relief, was shifted in the new cabinet to the justice department from the politically-hazardous economic growth portfolio. Appointed to economic growth was Lawrence Garvie, a 40-year-old Fredericton lawyer whose cautious, conciliatory manner had earned him the Speaker's chair in Hatfield's first government. Garvie spoke in slow, measured tones. In the months after his appointment, he would speak in even slower, more measured tones. Opposition members and reporters with questions about Bricklin would begin to believe they were attempting to pull teeth, not words, from him. In September, 1975, Garvie would make the recommendation to put Bricklin under.

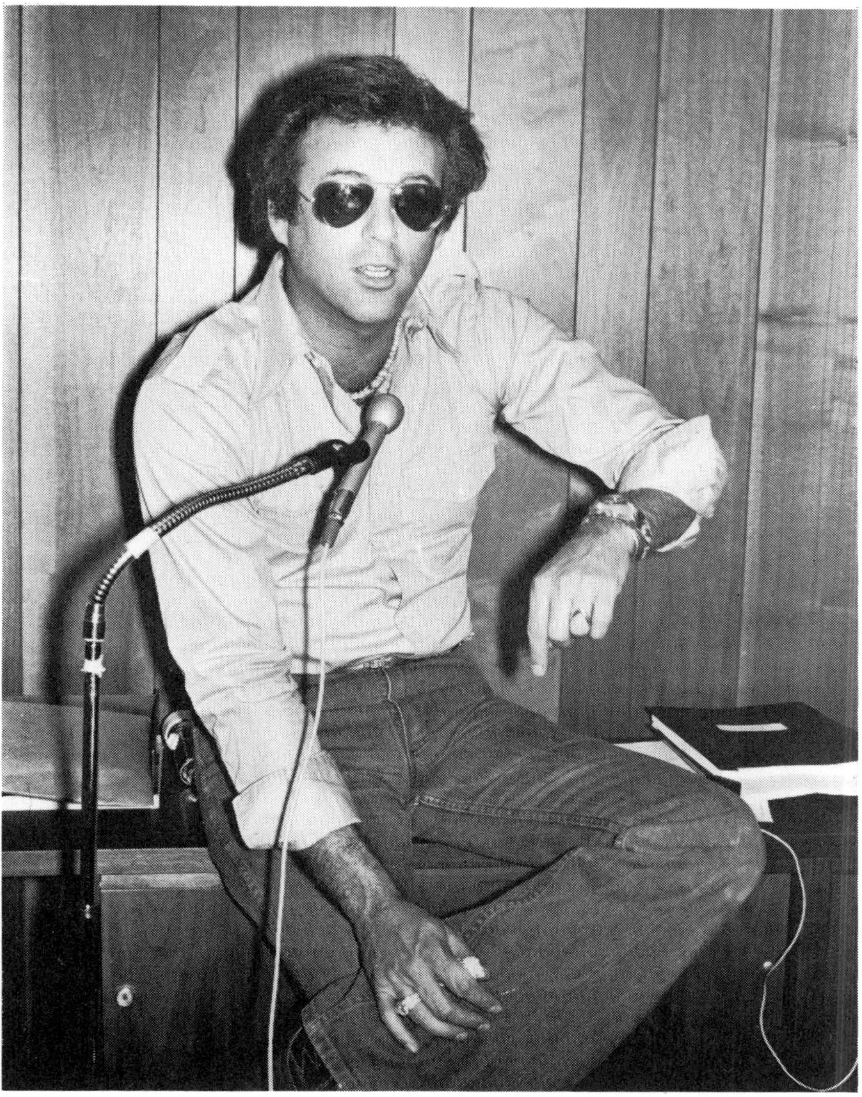

GEM Photos Reproductions Ltd., Saint John

Malcolm Bricklin

New Brunswick
Information Service →

Premier Richard Hatfield (left) *and Malcolm Bricklin, touring the Saint John plant.*

GEM Photos Reproductions Ltd., Saint John

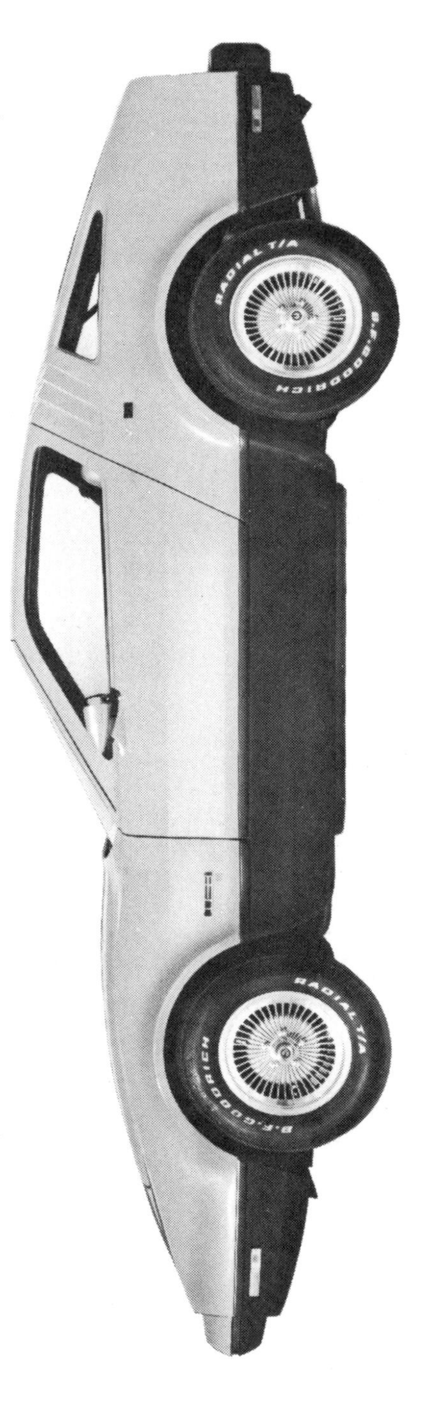

A prototype of the Bricklin car

GEM Photos Reproductions Ltd., Saint John

(Above) *The Saint John plant where Bricklin cars were assembled.* (Below) *Workers lay fibreglass in acrylic moulds at the Bricklin body-parts plant at Minto.*

The Daily Gleaner

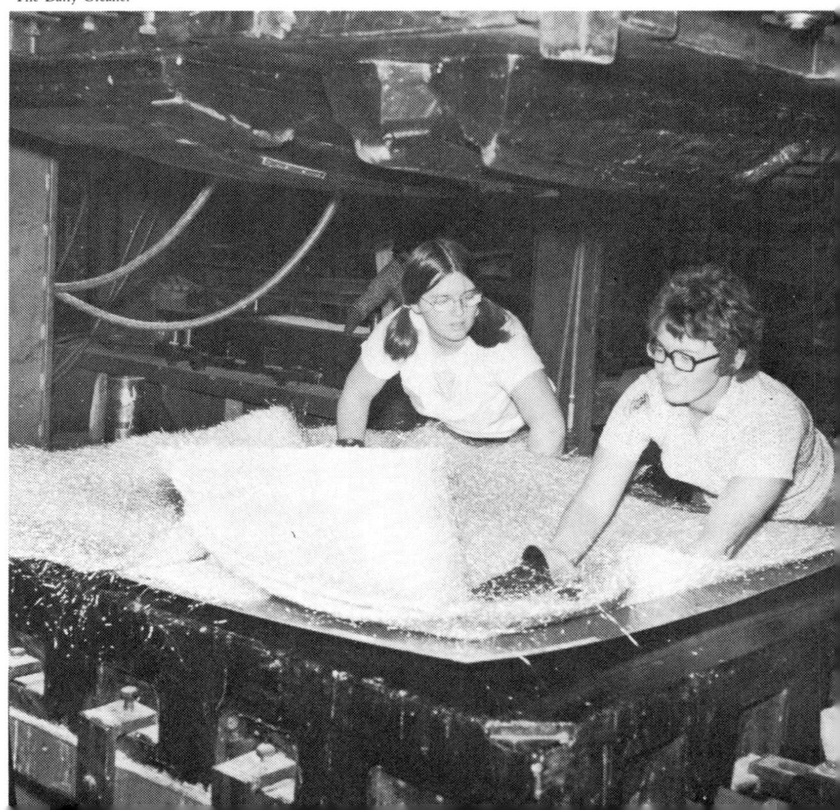

GEM Photos Reproductions Ltd., Saint John

(Above) *Albert Bricklin at work in the Saint John plant.* (Below) *A Bricklin car on the assembly line at Saint John.*

GEM Photos Reproductions Ltd., Saint John

Harvey Studios Ltd., Saint John

(Above) *A load of Bricklin cars for shipment to the U.S.* (Below) *Bricklin cars outside the Saint John plant.*

GEM Photos Reproductions Ltd., Saint John

The Daily Gleaner

Malcolm Bricklin, with cars on his shirt, at the Saint John plant. The driver is Hatfield.

Deanna Bradley, Woodstock Bugle

Charlie Russell (right), *a Woodstock, N.B., disc jockey, presents Hatfield with a copy of Russell's record,* 'The Bricklin and Other Sound Investments'.

Chapter 12

YES, MALCOLM — THERE IS A SANTA CLAUS

The Christmas season in New Brunswick is usually a tranquil time, even for politicians. The New Brunswick countryside, like that of New England, is thick with snow by mid-December. Christmas tree growers have put their firs and pines on sale in the towns and cities. In Fredericton, the government's large glass-walled office building is strung with lights and there is Christmas music in the lobby. It is a difficult time of year to reach a civil servant. From the street, the government building seems to sway slightly to the strains of the office parties inside. The government employees, who practise half-frowns for most of the year, are humming in the hallways. The 1974 Christmas season was like any other for them, except that nobody was humming in the offices of the department of economic growth and of the premier. Outside, the Bricklin controversy continued to rage. Hatfield would escape it only when he left for a holiday in Upper Volta in late December.

On December 4, following disclosures (through the publication of orders-in-council) that the government had approved financing of $2 million to Bricklin during the election, and not $1 million as Hatfield had indicated, the Opposition Liberals renewed their calls for a feasibility study of the project. "Without a cost feasibility study," Turnbull said in a prepared statement, "we are always going to have cabinet ministers guessing as to whether or not the company's operations will be viable and our jobs secure." At the same time, Higgins said in a statement that none of the estimated $1.2 million collected by Bricklin in dealership franchise fees had been returned to New Brunswick. "How can one reconcile Malcolm Bricklin asking for millions of dollars from New Brunswick for the Canadian company when, according to my information, the money for dealership or franchise sales remains in the United States?" he asked.

Meanwhile, reporters were seeking details of the purchase of the Simms' plant by the government — an issue that Turnbull declined to pursue because his law firm was representing Simms in the transaction. It was disclosed that the sale would take place on December 16, when legal forms were completed, and that the province would pay $1 million to Simms and take over a $540,000 mortgage held by the New Brunswick Development Corporation, a Crown agency, on the plant. The government would become both a landlord and its own tenant when the plant was purchased, since the province was the majority shareholder in Bricklin Canada Ltd., to which the plant was leased.

On December 12, Hatfield traveled to Saint John to address the local board of trade. The port city was aswirl with rumors and speculation about the Bricklin project. The board of trade had asked Hatfield to speak about economic development. The *Telegraph-Journal*, in an editorial published on the morning of his arrival, ventured the hope that he would talk about governments and business, and about the lengths to which a government should go "in bailing out industries in trouble." It was Hatfield's first official visit to Saint John since November 18, and he was aware of its significance. The city, the largest in the province, had voted heavily for the Liberals. It was now the centre of opposition to Hatfield's government, and to the Bricklin project.

Hatfield picked up the challenge. He insisted that his government would actively involve itself in development, despite the "definite risks." His government had entered directly into the management of the province's forests. It had provided heavy financing to the Saint John port, although the port was a federal responsibility. It had decided to proceed with the construction of a nuclear power plant near Saint John on its own, after the federal government had declined to provide the direct financing that it had given to Ontario and Quebec. Also, his government had committed itself to provide aid to secondary manufacturing industries, of which Bricklin was perhaps "the most dramatic example."

The assembled businessmen had been waiting for Hatfield to raise the Bricklin issue. They didn't have to wait any longer. "We cannot guarantee its (Bricklin's) success," he went on, "but I am convinced the attacks on it are premature, unfair, and prejudicial to its success." He responded to Liberal criticism. Liberal statements that cars were being sold to Bricklin's U.S. companies for $2,200 were "completely untrue." The transfer price was over $5,000 and the price of $2,200 contained in the June, 1973 agreement between the government and Bricklin had become "academic" because of rising costs. Statements that Bricklin's U.S. companies weren't returning franchise fees to New Brunswick were misleading. The money was used to support car design and sales in the U.S. In response to charges of mis-management, Hatfield said Clarkson Gordon & Company had been retained to monitor transfer prices and inter-company payments "and any matters they believe relevent to the government's interests." Also, Touche-Ross & Co. had been hired as Bricklin's auditors. Also, a task force of consultants would soon begin work on Bricklin's production problems.

Then Hatfield made an announcement. The government had decided to provide the additional $2.5 million in financing that

Bricklin had requested. The announcement left the room in utter silence. One could have heard a Rotary pin drop. Hatfield went on: "It has been said that the present government has a political stake in the success of the project. That is true, but in fact the political future of a government is almost always determined on the balance of its achievements and its shortcomings, rather than by any one project or policy."

Among those at the meeting was Turnbull, the Opposition's leading critic of Bricklin, and Hatfield took a swipe at him. "What dismays me," he said, "is that there is at least one politician in this city who has talked himself into a position where he has a political stake in the failure of the project. That is an unenviable, and unbecoming, position for any person who has the interests of New Brunswick at heart." By this time, the members of the board of trade were fiddling studiously with the crumbs on their plates. Hatfield closed with a plea that the Saint John business community "be not negative and fearful, but positive and confident" in its relations with his government. Then he wished them a merry Christmas.

The *Telegraph-Journal* was incensed. "When he (Hatfield) appeared in advertising promotions with the Bricklin in the background, the inference was that he was backing a winner," the newspaper said in an editorial the next day. "He was pictured as a winning politician who had brought the province a new industry. But he wasn't at that time saying that, by the way, the province had given the Bricklin another million just before the election or that we'd probably have to kick in a few more million after the election." The newspaper characterised Hatfield's announcement of new financing as a 'Merry Christmas, Malcolm' gift to Bricklin.

But the Saint John newspaper, in another editorial published the same day, was equally unkind to Turnbull, who had declined to discuss the government's purchase of the Simms' plant because his law firm, Palmer, O'Connell, Leger, Turnbull and Turnbull, was negotiating the sale on behalf of Simms. In an editorial entitled, 'Really, Mr. Turnbull,' the newspaper noted that Turnbull had been "the most vocal and the most severe critic" of Hatfield's handling of the Bricklin project. "Mr. Turnbull," the editorial continued, "has emerged as the hit man of the Liberal Party and in his statements righteous indignation has reigned supreme. He has demanded more information and he has said he is amazed that the Opposition has had to "dig out" facts about a company owned by the people of New Brunswick.

"Right on, John. Right on.

"Now how about the T. S. Simms deal? The provincial government has said it is about to buy the plant owned by T. S. Simms and Co. Ltd. where the Bricklin cars are being manufactured. The province then will rent the plant to the Bricklin company. The inference is that the Simms company needs the money, among other things, to refund DREE funds because it did not provide the jobs it had projected when it got the DREE grants.

"In these circumstances, would the province be making money available to be funnelled back to a federal agency which invested in the Simms' venture which failed to get off the ground? Impossible. But neither the premier nor the company will give details.

"But not to worry. The People's Choice is either in a telephone booth changing into his Superman suit or out back of the barn mounting his white charger. The sun never sets on the British Empire or the Loyal Opposition, or almost never.

"But, wait, is the sun about to go down? John Turnbull says he is going to pass on the Simms deal. He doesn't have any comment. Is it good or bad for the province? Is the investment justified? Does it make good business sense? Should the money be spent?

"But John Turnbull has gone mute. His law firm represents the Simms company. Someone else will have to mount the white charger this time.

"But that's your horse, John. You're the one who has been hammer and tongs after the premier. Now, more money is about to be spent in this complex Bricklin-Simms-Government deal. If it is a good deal for the province, say so and support the government. If it isn't a good deal, then get out of your conflict-of-interest position and say so, too. After all, how many hit men do the Liberals have for this kind of work?

"The public is not going to buy a courageous and self-righteous hero on a part-time basis, so this is the time to declare yourself or turn in your Superman suit.

"Or one of those hats."

Thus fueled, the Bricklin controversy continued to build in the days before Christmas. On December 16, the Liberals ran full-page advertisements in the province's daily newspapers — a tactic that, outside of election campaigns, hadn't been seen in New Brunswick since the Equal Opportunity debates of the 1960s. The advertisements, which included a photograph of Turnbull and a large-type statement, 'The people have the right to know all the facts,' repeated calls for a feasibility study of Bricklin. It accused the government of failing to act in the best interests of the province. It criticized Hatfield for proceeding through cabinet, and not through the New Brunswick Development Corporation, in his financing of Bricklin. Bricklin's backing wasn't researched adequately before the government invested in the promoter, it said. In the first year of Bricklin's operation, the government had taken no direct involvement in Bricklin hirings or spending. Bricklin was allowed to set up a U.S. marketing arm "under a separate chain of corporate ownership." The U.S. marketing arm had collected $1.2 million in franchise fees, which wasn't returned to New Brunswick.

The Liberal statement repeated accusations that Hatfield's actions in the November election campaign amounted to a "fraud on the people of New Brunswick." If, as he insisted, he had said during the campaign that Bricklin needed more money, it must have been when he had laryngitis, the statement said. It raised the suggestion that the $2 million direct loan to Bricklin in early October was used partially to meet bank repayments that Bricklin would otherwise have defaulted. The statement said that Bricklin's heavy debts, along with inflation and parts shortages, "cry out" for a feasibility study, and that the Liberals wouldn't accept public statements from Hatfield which amounted to "equal parts of conceit, triumph and disdain."

The uproar soon attracted reporters from outside New Brunswick, who flew in for a couple of days, read old news clippings and made telephone calls, and became instant skeptics. 'The Bricklin Car: Will They Call It Hatfield's Folly?' asked the *Toronto Star* in a December 21 headline. "New Brunswick," said the kicker over the headline, "is being drawn ever deeper into the financial problems of building promoter Malcolm Bricklin's dream car and the skeptics are having a field day." The *Star* gave a lengthy review of the Bricklin project's history and came to the surprising conclusion that the province, by negotiating a royalty share and purchasing GVI shares during the election campaign, could share in "any financial windfall" that might come to Bricklin. "Of course, if the venture flops, the bets are off," said the *Star*. *Weekend Magazine* ran a similar review under the five-layer headline, 'What happened when the premier of an unemployment-ridden province met a millionaire who wanted to build a sports car.' The magazine observed that, "Unemployment has become a way of life in many quarters of New Brunswick," and said that Bricklin had strode into "a setting of industrial failures" when he came to the province. *Weekend* came to the unsurprising conclusion that the 'fate' of the Bricklin car would likely be known before the next (1978) New Brunswick election.

In New Brunswick, the debate rolled on into the holiday season. Turnbull declined the *Telegraph-Journal's* invitation to step into the Simms' plant issue, but Higgins picked it up. He called for the release of documents relating to the plant's purchase. "Since the people of New Brunswick, through our government, are now landlord, tenant and first mortgagee, and since money from the people of New Brunswick is to be used to pay the rent and mortgage, surely we are entitled to seeing all documents relating to our latest acquisition," he said in a prepared statement. The government made no response. Meanwhile, Leroy Washburn, a Liberal back-bencher from Oromocto, heard rumors that the Minto plant would be closed, and hastily sent a telegram to the economic growth department (eight miles away) for clarification. The rumors were unfounded, and possibly Liberal-inspired, but before they were doused the people of New Brunswick were shaking their heads at yet another Bricklin development.

On December 23, a Philadelphia District Court jury ordered Malcolm Bricklin to pay $2.3 million to Leon Stern, the Pompano Beach businessman who had sued Bricklin in 1972 for breach-of-contract. Stern charged that Bricklin had not honored a 1971 oral agreement to make Stern a partner in a proposed chain of U.S. "leisure land" resorts, to which Stern had contributed a resort property that he owned in the Poconos. Instead, Stern claimed, Bricklin had used the property title as security for bank loans, and had not given Stern the $1,000-a-week salary and the shares in FasTrack Leisure Land Ltd. that Bricklin had promised. The Philadelphia jury, after a three-week trial, agreed with Stern.

Wire stories of the jury verdict reached New Brunswick's newsrooms on Christmas Eve, and were run prominantly in Boxing Day editions of the province's newspapers. Hatfield was unavailable for comment. He had departed for Upper Volta, a tiny African country. Bricklin was unavailable for comment. He was passing Christmas in a resort condominium he had rented in Aspen, Colorado. He had just announced that he would offer five Bricklin cars to the Scottsdale police force for promotional purposes. The police would lease the cars for $1 each. The Stern wire stories left a worrisome question. Would New Brunswick, through the complex chain of Bricklin companies, wind up paying Bricklin's breach-of-contract debt to Stern? On December 27, reporters obtained a reaction from Harry Nason, the province's deputy minister of economic growth. Nason said he believed that FasTrack International Inc. and FasTrack Leisure Land Inc., the two companies named in Stern's lawsuit, were "independent of the operation here." Would the jury verdict affect Bricklin's ability to raise money for the New Brunswck project? That's a good question, said Nason. He didn't know.

Another man who left New Brunswick for the Christmas holidays was Ian Watson, the young comptroller of Bricklin Canada Ltd. Watson took his family to Vermont. He had a lot of thinking to do. The 3,500 GVI shares that he had received when he joined Bricklin a year earlier were still only worth one cent apiece — it was not like getting in on the ground floor at General Motors after all. It appeared to Watson that Bricklin wouldn't last much longer. Most of the $2.5 million loan approved by the province before Christmas would have to be applied to existing debts. Bricklin needed more money, and, with the political controversy still swirling, it seemed unlikely that the province would advance more. Further, the company had only produced about 500 cars in its first five months of production. Most of these cars were incomplete. They had been shipped to dealers as showroom models, not for sale. In January, there would be new production problems. Bricklin would be changing over to Ford engines, which didn't require a catalytic converter, and it was uncertain whether the change could be made without expensive design alterations to the car. There were other problems. It was becoming apparent that Bricklin's marketing program in the U.S. was in jeopardy. Bricklin couldn't deliver cars, and dealers had begun to spread the word that he was bad news. Existing dealers were worried that they would lose car deposits, along with payments for parts and servicing that hadn't arrived, and that their $4,880 franchise fees would come to nothing. New prospects were simply drying up. Bricklin had intended, in the beginning, to develop his marketing program in the northeastern U.S., but he had soon roamed further afield in search of franchise fees. He now had dealers in over 40 states — an impossible area to service. Some of the states had only one or two dealers.

Watson had another concern. His job with Bricklin had begun to affect his family. His children were getting into arguments at school in Saint John over the Bricklin car. In December, the Bricklin was an almost daily topic of argument on radio phone-in shows. The comments were sometimes so negative that Watson's wife, Tina, would call the station to defend her husband's livelihood. Carol Scully, Vic Scully's wife, was doing the same thing.

Watson decided to resign. He returned to Saint John and collected a $4,000 bonus promised to him when he joined Bricklin. If he waited any longer, he thought, Bricklin might not be able to pay the bonus. Scully, Rose's protege, took over Watson's job.

Chapter 13

BRICKLIN TAKES A BACK SEAT

Since late 1974, Malcolm Bricklin had been under pressure from the First Pennsylvania Bank to improve the management of his companies. Bricklin's financial statements to the bank, which were required under the terms of his loans, were frequently out of date. Bricklin's companies were kiting cheques regularly. The bank was unhappy with the large number of Bricklin relatives and fellow-travelers on the Bricklin payroll. The bank, with over $5 million invested in Bricklin, wanted a tighter operation. Bricklin had attempted to calm the bank by playing musical chairs with his existing officers (The changes were so frequent at some stages that they are impossible to follow. Often they were made on the spur of the moment, and they weren't recorded in the minutes of directors' meetings. At one point, judging from public statements, Malcolm and Albert were both the president of Bricklin Canada Ltd. at the same time), but the bank wasn't satisfied. The bank, in fact, was beginning to adopt the position that it should enter directly into the management of some of the companies it financed. John Bunting, the president of the First Pennsylvania Bank, said as much in a late 1974 interview with *Newsweek*.

In late 1974, Bricklin began to look for a new president of Bricklin Canada Ltd. (It is still uncertain whom the new president, when he was found, would replace. Malcolm Bricklin would announce that he was being replaced. However, Bricklin officials in Saint John believed that Albert Bricklin was the president of Bricklin Canada Ltd. That is what Albert told them). What sort of president, Bricklin wondered, would satisfy the First Pennsylvania Bank? Bricklin developed a list of prospects. He discussed his list with Joseph Rose, his chief financial adviser, over the 1974 Thanksgiving weekend. The list included Ralph Henry, a senior vice-president of the First Pennsylvania Bank, who had represented the bank on the Bricklin project from the beginning. Rose looked over the list. He had an idea that Bricklin would pick Henry. In December, 1974, Bricklin asked Henry if he would be the president of Bricklin Canada Ltd. and General Vehicle Inc. They began to negotiate. Henry said he would do it. The bank was satisfied. In late December, the New Brunswick government was informed of Henry's appointment. New Brunswick officials, including Garvie, had traveled to New York and Philadelphia in late December for financial meetings with officials of the First Pennsylvania Bank. The government was satisfied with Henry's appointment.

On January 9, 1975, Bricklin and Henry traveled to Toronto to view a pre-screening of *The Bricklin Story,* a film produced in 1974 by In-Sight Productions of Toronto, with the help of $10,000 from Bricklin. The film would be shown nationally the following night on the Canadian Broadcasting Corporation's *Gallery* series. It amounted to thirty minutes of fawning over Bricklin. He was shown on his Arizona ranch, riding his horse, driving his car, philosophizing on the corral fence with a cowboy hat tilted back on his head. The camera followed a Bricklin car into the sunset. Bricklin ruminated in a voice-over about the meaning of success and failure. Hatfield had a minute or two in the film and said he had a gut feeling about Bricklin. After its television showing, the film would be panned royally by Toronto reviewers. Dennis Braithwaite, for example, would complain in the *Toronto Star* that he had wanted to learn something about the Bricklin car project, but was given only "trendy shots of a dude riding his horse into the setting sun." He would describe the film as "television puff."

During the Toronto visit, Bricklin held a press conference to announce the appointment of Henry as the new president of Bricklin Canada Ltd. and General Vehicle Inc. Bricklin would become chairman of the two companies. He denied that he was being forced out. "A lot of people are going to say, 'Aha, Malcolm Bricklin's being pushed aside.' Well I'm pushing myself aside," Bricklin said. "I was able to convince people who know how to do these things, which I don't, that the Bricklin could be built. That's as far as I go. That's where my talents stop." Henry told the press conference that he had severed all ties with the First Pennsylvania Bank. He was certain the Bricklin project would succeed. "The fact that I would leave my job to join Malcolm Bricklin is an indication of my confidence in the venture. There is no question in my mind that this will be a success." Bricklin also announced that the retail price of his car would rise again, but that it would remain below $10,000. He also announced that he still needed another $4 million to $5 million in the next few months. His money-raising efforts outside New Brunswick had not been successful.

After the press conference, Bricklin and Henry flew to Montreal to attend an international car show at the Bonaventure Hotel, in which the Bricklin car was entered. In an effort to calm dealer fears about his car, Bricklin had placed Tony Kopp, a long-time associate and director of public relations with GVI, in charge of a series of Bricklin car appearances at automobile shows across the continent in 1975. Celebrities such as Art Linkletter and Donald Nixon would agree to attend the shows. In January and February, the Bricklin car would appear in shows in San Francisco, Los Angeles, New York, Toronto and Montreal. By then, Kopp, who also ran Bricklin's Phoenix raceway, would be gone. He and Alan Salke, an early financial adviser to Bricklin, were two people the First Pennsylvania Bank wanted to remove from the Bricklin operation. Both would insist later that they left because they could see that Bricklin was sinking.

On January 10, Bricklin and Henry flew to Saint John. Bricklin introduced Henry to the Bricklin Canada Ltd. board of directors. The directors had not approved the hiring of Henry, and would never get around to doing so. Although they held ostensible control over the Bricklin operation, according to loan conditions established by the province, they were an ineffectual presence. Wheatley and Wallace Turnbull, who is a cousin of John Turnbull's, but whose first loyalty is to the Conservative party, were the two provincial nominees to the board. Bricklin's appointees were himself, Albert, and Joseph Rose.

In Saint John, Bricklin also introduced Henry to the local media on January 10. In an interview with the *Telegraph-Journal,* Henry said it had become clear to him that Bricklin needed an operational head. "I recognized that someone had to come in here in that position, for the best interests of everyone," he said. He rejected suggestions that his appointment was a move by the First Pennsylvania Bank, where he had worked for twenty-six years, to protect its own interests. "I'm the one that decided I wanted to join Mr. Bricklin," he said. "No one in the bank ever suggested that." Bricklin said in the same interview that the $2.3 million judgment awarded to Leon Stern in December had nothing to do with the Bricklin companies. He also said the judge in the case was so upset with the jury verdict that he refused to allow a judgment to be placed — an assertion that Judge Raymond Broderick, who heard the case, would subsequently deny. In another interview with a local CBC reporter the same day, Bricklin denied that he was being forced out of his companies, although he said there had been pressure to find a new president for the companies' day-to-day operations. "There was pressure from day one to find a man," he said. "If it's interpreted that the bank or the province, you know, insisted on it, I don't . . . " Bricklin also said he was having trouble in raising the $4 million to $5 million he thought his companies needed. "Right now, we are scouring various places, as we have been for some time. The difficulty there is, the press has been asking the questions . . . They (investors) are pressured by the fact that the press keeps asking, is it going to make it."

After the round of introductions, Ralph Henry, the fifty-four-year-old Philadelphia banker who had once built a Bradley kit car, settled into his new career as an automobile company president. While he intended to divide his time between Detroit and Saint John, he moved into a house in Saint John's fashionable Rothesay area. The rent of $600 a month was paid by Bricklin Canada Ltd. At the Bricklin plant, Henry was confronted by the same sort of problems that had driven earlier Bricklin personnel to distraction. He would be the first man since Hennessey to attempt to take charge of the entire Bricklin operation, and, in some measure, he would be successful. One result would be the virtual fading away from the picture of Joseph Rose, Bricklin's chief financial adviser. Henry would insist upon control over financial matters. Henry, not Rose, would approach the New Brunswick government for new financing. But Henry, like his predecessors, would make little headway with the production problems that continued to drive Bricklin deeper into debt. At the time of his arrival, for example, the plant was in the midst of an expensive changeover to Ford engines. Unlike the American Motors engines the company had been using, the Ford engines didn't require catalytic converters to meet new U.S. exhaust emission standards. But the problems of changing over had been under-estimated. Bricklin personnel were just discovering that they would have to make substantial design changes. The Bricklin frame would have to be altered, resulting in balance problems between the car's front and rear axles, which would have to be corrected. The entire subframe would have to be re-designed.

Henry was also given a quick introduction to labor problems at the Saint John plant. Shortly before his arrival, Bricklin had laid off 150 workers while the engine changeover was taking place. The day before Henry set foot in Saint John, the remaining workers at the plant had walked out over jurisdictional and grievance issues that union officials attributed to poor management. They returned to work quickly, but James Gilliland, a union official, complained to reporters that "the plant morale is almost negligible." The workers, like everyone else in Saint John, were prey to the unending rumors that Bricklin was on the verge of collapse. Within the plant, there were frequent rumors before each payday that Bricklin couldn't meet his payroll.

There were other headaches, such as the Saint John *Telegraph-Journal* which was becoming more critical daily of the Bricklin project. On the day after Henry's arrival, the newspaper noted in an editorial that Bricklin was having extraordinary success in exposing his car in magazines "with those naked ladies" (a reference to recent Bricklin publicity in *Playboy, Penthouse* and *Gallery*). But, the newspaper went on, Bricklin's financial affairs were "less of an open centrefold." Noting Henry's arrival, it posed "the five-million dollar question: where will Malcolm Bricklin go to get that extra $4 to $5 million he now says he needs to meet operational requirements? To *Playboy* publisher Hugh Hefner?"

Three days later, on January 14, the newspaper gleefully roasted *The Bricklin Story,* the film that had just been shown nationally on CBC television. "There he was, Old Mal, right up there on the television screen," said the newspaper's lead editorial, "perched on the old corral with his ten-gallon hat at a jaunty angle and sipping his sarsaparilla, and telling us that as a kid he had always wanted to be a cowboy. Now he was grown up and he had made a million dollars before he was twenty-five and he could be a cowboy whenever he wanted to, and he could ride off into the sunset on his horse, which he did, or he could ride off into the sunset in his Bricklin, which he did too. Talk about your all-American success stories." And people believed in "this boy," the newspaper went on. His mother and his father and the bankers believed. "And Richard Hatfield believed and pretty soon he came on the screen himself and smiled that confident smile and gave you that look that he uses when he is telling you about his own word being good, and he said he believed in Malcolm Bricklin and this was, well, just a gut feeling. That's what he called it. He was responsible to the people of New Brunswick and he had to determine on his own whether he was dealing with a con artist or a real honest-to-goodness entrepreneur, and he had decided — it was a gut determination, he said — but he had decided that Malcolm Bricklin was an entrepreneur. So the people of New Brunswick should feel good about that — if you can just imagine that eyeball-to-eyeball confrontation before the premier's gut told him that Old Mal was all right."

The editorial wound to a withering conclusion. "So here you have one of the great promotional geniuses of our time, and what he lacks in business acumen, why he makes up in, ah, entrepreneurship. Why, when Old Mal started out with this venture he had estimated that the Bricklin car would be in production in a matter of months, which showed just how much he knew about the business, he confided, and then he thought he could bring it on stream with an investment of about $3,000,000 which also showed you what a dreamer he was. But people believed and when he ran out of money, why, he just asked for more, and the banks and Richard Hatfield just came up with more money. It was real heart-warming."

Henry must have wondered about the Saint John paper. But he had other things to wonder about in the days after his arrival in Saint John. Bricklin was out of money. The company had cheques out that it couldn't cover. Bricklin himself could raise no money from private investors. The First Pennsylvania Bank, Henry knew, was not prepared to raise its investment. It had gone to the limit. That left the New Brunswick government.

The New Brunswick government was prepared to loan more money. It viewed Henry's arrival with some relief. He had a solid financial background. The government also believed that its production consultants, Wespac Development Planning Corp. Ltd., which had gone on the job in early January, would provide a measure of control. Garvie, the new economic growth minister, was prepared to advance substantial financing on the belief that, with controls in place, the company would be able finally to shake off its troublesome parts supply and production problems, and move onto a surer footing.

Henry and Garvie held meetings in January to discuss the large block of financing that Bricklin needed. The Wespac company was assigned by Garvie to prepare production goals and to establish a reliable reporting system between Bricklin and the government. Clifford Sawyer, a former Ford executive with links to the Conservative party, and Guy Campbell, another former automotive executive, were assigned by Wespac to monitor the Bricklin project. They would receive a per diem rate plus expenses from the government. In mid-January, the Conservative cabinet began to discuss Bricklin's money needs.

The January discussions went forward with an air of urgency. The $2.5 million loan to Bricklin in December had already been spent, largely to cover debts incurred before the money was even advanced. By mid-January, Bricklin was out of money again and beginning to float cheques. To give the company and itself room to manoeuvre while new financing was considered, the cabinet advanced an additional $1 million to Bricklin on January 23. The money was so badly needed that Vic Scully, the new comptroller of Bricklin Canada Ltd., had to interrupt a flight that afternoon from Saint John to Montreal in order to meet with government officials at the Fredericton airport, where he signed documents for the $1 million. The documents were brought to the airport by David Jennings, an economic growth employee. Bev Smith, a justice department employee, accompanied Jennings and witnessed Scully's signature. Then Scully flew on to Montreal. Jennings quickly forwarded the $1 million advance to the Bank of Montreal in Saint John. The money had to be in the bank the same day to cover outstanding cheques.

On January 30, Hatfield announced that his cabinet had agreed to "offer" new financing of $7.5 million to Bricklin. He didn't say that Bricklin had already accepted and spent $1 million of the $7.5 million offer. Hatfield said in a short, prepared statement that the new financing was needed to put Bricklin on a viable footing. The money would enable the company to ride out its production problems and reach a break-even level of production, which was estimated at 30 cars per day, he said. In return for its financing, the government would take the majority position on Bricklin Canada Ltd.'s board of directors, and would "increase its managerial involvement" in Bricklin's U.S. companies, Hatfield said. He said that preliminary advice given to the government by the Wespac consultants was "encouraging and supportive." The consultants would continue to monitor the Bricklin project. He also said the government didn't expect to invest further in Bricklin, "nor does it expect any further requests from the company for financial assistance from the province."

The terms of the new financing would not be settled in a written agreement until March 11. By that time they would be largely academic. Bricklin would have already received $2.9 million, or more than one-third, of the advance. The first $1 million was advanced on January 23. The next $1 million was advanced on February 13. Another $900,000 was advanced on March 4, a week before the agreement was signed. The agreement would not be made public until December 17, 1975, by which time it would be wholly academic. Bricklin would have been in receivership for three months.

The agreement signed on March 11, 1975, would represent the government's first concerted attempt to take control of the Bricklin project. It would run to seventeen pages and it would consist largely of terms and qualifiers meant to inhibit Malcolm Bricklin and to protect the province. The agreement would provide for an increase from five members to seven on the Bricklin Canada Ltd. board of directors, with the province appointing four of the seven directors. The $7.5 million loan would be used as working capital for the Saint John and Minto plants, "and for no other purpose." Malcolm Bricklin would be required to devote his "full time and attention" to the Bricklin project.

The agreement would accord recognition to two of Bricklin's new dreams in the spring of 1975. He wanted to begin research on another car, and he wanted to begin research on an alternative power train. The March 11 agreement would attempt to establish some control over each of these projects. According to its terms, Bricklin would have to postpone the projects until his U.S. companies were making profits of $500,000 "in any continuous period." In the summer of 1975, Bricklin would simply ignore these terms. He had already established Bricklin Power Supply Ltd. to develop a new engine. (In late 1975, less than three months after the collapse of Bricklin Canada Ltd., Bricklin would announce that he was promoting a "revolutionary new engine," but he would say that New Brunswick funds had nothing to do with the engine). In the summer of 1975, Bricklin would instruct two design engineers to begin work at Livonia on a new Bricklin luxury car, to be called the Bricklin Chairman. The engineers would be paid by Bricklin Canada Ltd.

The March 11 agreement would re-assert the province's right to examine the accounting records, including records of car transfer payments and documents, of all the Bricklin companies. The province had held the right since the signing of the June, 1973, agreement, but had not exercised it. The March 11 agreement would further stipulate that a transfer price for cars would be established that would allow Bricklin Canada Ltd. to make a clear profit of $100 on each car.

There would be other terms intended to harness Bricklin. He would not be able to build a plant elsewhere unless Bricklin's U.S. companies purchased the first 12,000 cars a year from Saint John. Bricklin Canada Ltd. could not be re-organized or wound up before the loan was repaid. (This was a curious term. It was intended to prevent Bricklin from escaping his obligations, but Bricklin would use it as the basis for a possible lawsuit in 1976 after the province had put Bricklin Canada Ltd. in receivership). Another term in the agreement would require that FasTrack International Inc. subordinate its royalties on Bricklin cars (Bricklin had tied in FasTrack to the Bricklin companies in anticipation of profits to come) until the $7.5 million loan had been repaid. Bricklin patents and trademarks would be transferred to Bricklin Canada Ltd. — clearly an effort to prevent Bricklin from going into business elsewhere. Also, the province would be given warrants on two million shares of GVI stock, which represented one-quarter of the U.S. company's stock.

Other terms of the agreement would provide for personal guarantees by Malcolm Bricklin, which were worthless, and for the weekly reporting of production figures and projections to the government — as late as March, 1975, the government was still seeking reliable production figures.

The March 11 agreement would not be signed by Joseph Rose, who had negotiated the earlier agreements on behalf of Bricklin. Ralph Henry would sign the March 11 agreement on behalf of Bricklin Canada Ltd. He would also sign on behalf of General Vehicle Inc., as president. He would also sign on behalf of Bricklin Vehicle Corp., Bricklin Northeast, Inc., Bricklin Midwest, Inc., and Bricklin Power Supply Ltd. He had become a director of these companies.

Hatfield's January 30 announcement was greeted, predictably, by protests. Turnbull, the Liberals' Bricklin critic, accused the government of complete contempt for the province's taxpayers. "I hope it is a lesson that will not be forgotten by the people of New Brunswick," he said, and repeated calls for a feasibility study.

Coincidently, the Atlantic Provinces Economic Council (APEC), an organization that conducts economic research in the Atlantic Provinces, released a report on the same day as Hatfield's announcement in which it warned of a "fateful similarity" between the government's involvement in Bricklin and the earlier involvement of the Nova Scotia government in Clairtone Industries Ltd., an electronics firm that collapsed after receiving heavy public investment. "Clairtone in the past, and Bricklin now, rely on parts brought in from long distances and on markets equally far removed," said the report, which was written for APEC by Lyndon Watkins, a Halifax freelance writer and former Atlantic Provinces reporter for *The Globe and Mail.* "Its (Bricklin's) reason for being in New Brunswick is the availability of government financing and an adequate labor supply."

Hatfield reacted angrily to the report. APEC was uninformed, he told a reporter. "Surely they realize a large part of the Bricklin is coming from Minto," he said. It wasn't APEC's business to criticize government development policies, he said. "Society doesn't need professional crepe-hangers." He also insisted, in response to a reporter's questions, that he had found little evidence of skepticism in New Brunswick over Bricklin, "except for a couple of MLAs and a couple of editorial writers, and I'm not impressed with the credentials of either of them." He took swipes at Turnbull, predicting the Saint John MLA would disappear if the Bricklin issue disappeared. "He doesn't have anything else to say about anything, about Saint John, or social issues, or any issues. I think he's riding a hobby horse, and let him ride it." Hatfield also insisted the Bricklin project appeared to be a success, although "not for eternity, not even the Bank of Canada can claim that, or the *Telegraph-Journal.*"

While Hatfield was attacking Bricklin's critics, Malcolm Bricklin was taking potshots of his own in Saint John, where he had agreed to speak to members of the local press club on February 1, two days after the announcement of new financing. Bricklin, who had just returned from a New York auto show where he announced a price increase to $9,980 for his car, accused the New Brunswick press of weakening "investor confidence" in the car. "You're beginning to cost me a lot of money," he told the Saint John reporters. "You're discouraging a lot of businesses that want to come to New Brunswick." The reporters would joke later that the province couldn't afford many more businesses like Bricklin. "New Brunswick," Bricklin theorized, "is self-deprecating. They've never had any successful ventures. They perpetuate this. They say something won't work until eventually it doesn't."

Bricklin himself was experiencing no feelings of self-deprecation. In late 1974, he had met Michael Avery, a sort of lifestyles expert who gave courses to West Coast businessmen on the powers of positive thinking. Bricklin had encountered Avery at a California love-in, to which he had taken Colleen McCabe, his girlfriend and future wife. In coming months, Bricklin and Avery would become a sort of walking T-group. Avery, who was in his late twenties, would coach Bricklin on the dynamics of interacting with Garvie, the economic growth minister, and Clifford Sawyer, the tough-minded Wespac consultant, both of whom intimidated Bricklin in some degree. When Avery visited Saint John, he would announce to workers at the Bricklin plant that it was "motivation day." Avery would move quickly onto Bricklin's payroll, as 'assistant to the chairman', at a salary of $24,000. At the time of Bricklin's collapse in September, 1975, Avery would be slated to become the president of Bricklin Vehicle Corporation, at a salary of $90,000. Avery, with his motivation lectures, would bring Bricklin back from despondency over the collapse.

Chapter 14

ROUGH AND TUMBLE TIME

The New Brunswick legislature is a lovable, domed mongrel of a building, all sandstone and pomp. By March, when the annual spring session begins, the building's copper roof is weighted down with about two feet of melting snow, which gives an air of imminent disaster. The Speech from the Throne is read to the sounds of crashing ice. Inside, the building's hallways are hung with the staid, dark-toned portraits of former lieutenant-governors. Reporters who are late for prayers can stand in the hallway and gaze at Lord Glenelg on the wall, and spell his name backwards and forwards. After prayers, the proceedings inside the assembly are sometimes not very staid. Members openly refer to one another with nicknames like Pipsqueak, Jaws and Bozo. Cabinet ministers have been known to reel in the hallways, under Lord Glenelg, or at their desks while speaking. William Woodroffe, the Speaker of the present assembly, has been driven to the point of admonishing members not to pop peanuts, shout insults, or take off their shoes during debates in the House. The proceedings seem to deteriorate as spring wears on. By May, Rodman Logan, the province's towering, grey-haired labor minister, is usually on his feet to interrupt proceedings with his Diefenbaker imitations.

The Speech from the Throne opening the first session of the 48th New Brunswick legislature was read on March 11, 1975, the same day the government signed an agreement covering a loan of $7.5 million to Bricklin. On March 12, the day after the opening, Turnbull presented a lengthy notice of motion seeking documents related to the financing and operations of Bricklin Canada Ltd. and its associated companies. The notice of motion asked for minutes of directors' meetings, copies of expenditures and inter-company invoices, budgets, government and bank correspondence, and agreements dating back to June, 1973, when the government made its first investment in Bricklin. The Liberals knew the government was unlikely to release the documents, but they believed that public opinion was moving against the Bricklin project, and they were prepared to capitalize on it by debating for days. The Liberals were also moving closer to a resolution within their own party of differing positions toward the Bricklin issue. A growing number of caucus members was beginning to agitate for a wholesale condemnation of the project.

On March 25, Turnbull's motion came up on the order paper. The government intended to vote it down. The Liberals prepared for a long debate, hoping to embarrass the government. Turnbull, one of the few members of the assembly who doesn't speak from a prepared text, began the debate by accusing the government, through its manoeuvres with the Bricklin plants at Saint John and Minto, of having put the province "in the ludicrous situation where we are landlord, tenant, mortgagor and mortgagee." Then he launched into a description of what he called "the ripoff aspects" of the Bricklin project. "The game of musical chairs is being played with the management of the company," he said. "We have corporate shells springing up all over the place . . . We have a situation where New Brunswick taxpayers own 67 per cent of a company. We have another company, General Vehicle Inc. in Delaware with issued capital of over 5,000,000 shares, of which New Brunswick has an option on 400,000 shares (Turnbull wasn't aware that New Brunswick had taken options on two million GVI shares in the March 11 agreement). I don't even know if that option has been exercised yet, but if it has, we own about one-tenth, one-eleventh or one-twelfth of the company.

"One of the first things that anyone learns in business," he went on, "is that where you have a half pocket with a whole pocket watching, the whole pocket will be billing the half pocket and the whole pocket is going to get rich. Everybody knows that, and that is the situation we are into here. The whole pocket is selling the franchises, but believe me, there are going to be no franchises, there are going to be no dealers unless our company, Bricklin Canada Ltd., produces cars. However, as I said, the franchises or the dealerships are being sold and that money is going into the promoter's whole pocket. Then we have many bills that have been received by our New Brunswick company from the whole pocket . . . "

Turnbull went on to present a series of questions that he said couldn't be answered unless the documents requested in his motion were made public. What was the nature of inter-company dealings in the Bricklin organization? Did the car transfer arrangements in the June, 1973 agreement include payment to Bricklin Canada Ltd. for overhead, wages and bank interest, which weren't mentioned in the agreement? What happened at directors' meetings? Anything? What was the breakdown on 'special travel' costs of $412,061 charged to Bricklin Canada Ltd. for the period ending October 31, 1974? "Is the Opposition not to get a breakdown, but just to sit here like dummies?" he asked.

Garvie, the economic growth minister, got up. Since the 1974 election, the Conservative caucus had adopted the strategy of treating the Bricklin project publicly like any other government-financed industry in New Brunswick. The government would stick closely to this strategy in coming months, insisting that the Bricklin companies, like others in the province, had a right to privacy in their internal affairs. In the legislature, the government would insist that Liberal questions about Bricklin were irresponsible. Garvie, responding to Turnbull's questions, said only that the release of information demanded by the Liberals would threaten the Bricklin project "in the marketplace," as it would threaten other companies subjected to similar scrutiny. The government had to act prudently, he said. It would not release the information.

Andre Robichaud, a short ("Stand up when you speak," Logan, the labor minister, once growled at him. "I'm sorry, you are standing.") Liberal with a penchant for antagonizing the government members, launched a rambling response intended largely to waste time until the House adjourned, allowing the Liberals to prepare speeches for the next day. Robichaud said it seemed to him that the Bricklin corporate structure was a "setup to pump money out of New Brunswick." The whole thing smelled fishy, he said. "Is it true that we are being victimized, that we are being conned?" he asked. He began to single out government members. "I am sure my friend Omer (Leger), the minister of fisheries, would like to know a lot more about this matter. I am sure that the minister of finance (Edison Stairs), judging from the funny expression on his face, would like to know all the details of this matter . . ." Robichaud rambled on until the adjournment.

On March 26, the Liberals resumed their attack. They intended to pursue the debate throughout the day, raising questions and reaping publicity from the government's refusal to disclose information. The Liberal and Conservative party whips had made a tentative arrangement for the debate to end in the evening. Alan Graham, a Liberal frontbencher from Kent County, began the Liberal harangue. "Has there been a ripoff or has there been a sting performed on New Brunswick?" he asked. He said Bricklin needed a province like New Brunswick to finance his car, "but I am not so sure whether New Brunswick now needs Bricklin."

Graham was followed by Frank Branch, a large Liberal backbencher raised on rural speech-making and given to hyperbole (Branch's Gloucester County constituents do not live in poverty, they live in diabolical squalor). "The government comes on with the smokescreen," shouted Branch, warming up. "Are they smokescreeners or are they Conservatives, or are the two things synonymous?" Branch said it was his belief "that the government hopes that their neglect and smokescreening will come to a head at this time and be forgotten, fade into the fog." He warned that the province was becoming a dictatorship. "For years to come, governments will refer to the Garvie principle, the Garvie precedent of 1975, which is," he paused, then roared, "hammer down the lid!" Did the government members know what was happening? he asked. "They can say what they wish, but the look on the faces of the members on the government benches is that of Cleopatra, not when Mark Antony came into her tent, but just a few minutes after she was poisoned."

Before the supper hour, Hatfield entered the debate. He would close it for the government side, defending the position that Garvie had taken. In an attempt to take some of the sting out of the Liberal attacks, he would announce a new industrial disclosure policy — a set of guidelines restricting the information the government would release about any industry it assisted, including Bricklin. Hatfield began by describing Turnbull's motion as an "unprecedented" demand for information that is normally considered by companies to be confidential. Then he set the stage for his policy announcement. The type of information sought by the Liberals could threaten the government's entire development program, he said. It could lead to uncertainty among prospective investors, "and damage the business climate in this province." Hatfield said he was going to end the uncertainty the Liberals were creating. He would ensure that companies that received government assistance were treated in the same manner as any other private company. Government-financed companies would be required to reveal no more about themselves than private companies were required to disclose. The province's Companies Act would apply to both. (Hatfield didn't spell it out, but a company in New Brunswick is required to make public, in a yearly return, its list of officers, its head office and its authorized capitalization. Ironically, while Hatfield was making his policy statement, the government was considering a report by the justice department's law reform division that urged a reform of the province's antiquated company laws, particularly to provide for greater disclosure of business activities. The report was subsequently pigeon-holed).

Hatfield then proceeded to define the amount of information the government would release about its investments in companies. The government would name any company that received assistance. It would also disclose the amount of assistance, the nature of the assistance (whether a loan or guarantee), the number of jobs involved, and the product to be manufactured. But specific agreements between the government and a company (for example, the June, 1973, agreement between the government and Bricklin) would not be made public without the consent of the company involved. "Companies must compete in the marketplace," said Hatfield. "Political interference with management, and disclosure of information that other companies can keep confidential can make it impossible for government-supported companies to compete and survive."

Hatfield went on to accuse the Liberals of making Bricklin a political issue. He said his own use of a Bricklin in the 1974 campaigns was in response to Liberal whisperings. "Yes, Mr. Speaker, I was involved in a by-election campaign, and when the word was going around in that by-election that the premier couldn't drive his toy car at night because the lights didn't work, I said, All right, if they want to criticize the Bricklin, if they want to spread stories about it and try to discredit it, I will prove otherwise, so I brought a Bricklin into the by-election campaign to show people."

Over Liberal heckling, Hatfield accused the Opposition members of attempting to destroy the Bricklin company. "You say you are not against the Bricklin project, that you want to see Bricklin succeed, that all you want is public disclosure, all you want is accountability, and yet you spend the time of this House attacking an individual who happens to be the man who started the company, whose idea it was, whose idea has obviously — surely nobody denies it — received a great deal of public acceptance." How long would the Liberal criticisms continue? Hatfield asked. "It will go on for five years," he said, "for ten years or for fifteen years. It will go on until they are satisfied they have done everything they can possibly do to destroy the Bricklin project, to undermine confidence in it, to raise doubts."

The Liberals responded to Hatfield's attacks with a flurry of speeches that lasted into the night. The speeches were futile. With midnight approaching, Turnbull stood up to close the debate.

"There are people in the United States who claim they have been swindled by Malcolm Bricklin," Turnbull said. He listed claimants, including Robert Kohlman, Lawrence Fish, Vernon Fish, Harold Hassel, and James Bair, who had launched court actions against Bricklin and Handyman America, Inc. in 1964, shortly before the hardware chain was put into bankruptcy. He also listed Leon Stern, who had won a $2.3 million breach-of-contract lawsuit against Bricklin in 1974. "I see the same disquieting corporate setup here that was present with Handyman America, Inc.," Turnbull said. He then proceeded to table the Handyman court documents, creating a small stir among the government members, most of whom had not been aware of the lawsuits. "Mr. Premier," Turnbull said, "you and the cabinet have got us into this and you are embarrassing the great people of New Brunswick." Turnbull asked for a recorded vote. On party lines, the government defeated Turnbull's motion. The House adjourned.

The members of the New Brunswick legislature headed home for the Easter holiday. The province now had a new industrial disclosure policy. Controversy over Malcolm Bricklin's car had driven the government into a posture of greater secrecy in all its dealings with industry.

On April 9, less than two weeks after the Bricklin debate in the legislature, Garvie and Harry Nason, the deputy economic growth minister, met with Bricklin and Ralph Henry at the Lord Beaverbrook Hotel. Garvie had begun to receive reports from Clarkson Gordon and the Wespac consultants that production costs were running persistently higher than the cost at which Bricklin Canada Ltd. was transferring cars to General Vehicle Inc. Garvie instructed Bricklin and Henry to raise the transfer price from $5,400 per car to $7,200. After the meeting, a reporter questioned Garvie. "It was a routine meeting," Garvie said. Bricklin said in response to a reporter's questions that he was not thinking of asking the government for more money.

On April 22, Bricklin, conventionally dressed in a suit with a wool vest, made a speech to Fredericton businessmen at a meeting held in the Legion building. The speech represented the beginnings of an unofficial public relations campaign that Bricklin and Henry had decided to launch in hopes of countering the vigorous political debate over the car company. Bricklin told the Fredericton businessmen that his company was overcoming the bugs that had slowed production. The company was edging towards a break-even point. But Bricklin wished people would stop making a political issue of his car, and would get behind him and support the project. To get his car out of the "political arena," Bricklin said he was prepared to open his books to the New Brunswick Liberal party, if the Liberals would agree not to disclose what they saw. The following day, the Liberals declined his offer. Higgins said the Liberals "flatly rejected any type of secret meeting whatsoever."

The Liberals continued to raise questions in the remaining weeks of the spring session, but there were few responses. Garvie used the new disclosure policy to ward off the questions that Turnbull rained on him. For example, Garvie revealed during debate on his department's spending estimates in early June that the government had purchased two million shares from General Vehicle Inc., but he refused to name the purchase price, or the total number of shares that General Vehicle had issued. "That's a private company," said Garvie. "I can't disclose that." In fact, the government had paid one cent apiece for the shares. General Vehicle had authorized capital of eight million shares.

Chapter 15

THE BREAK-EVEN CAMPAIGN

The divergence between what Bricklin said about his car (the promotion) and what was actually happening (the business) became complete in the summer of 1975. Before then, there had always been some tenuous link, even if it was only an admission by Bricklin that his projections were lousy. By the summer of 1975, there wasn't even a link. Bricklin launched a publicity campaign to convince the people of New Brunswick that his companies were at a break-even point, were making a cash profit, and would soon begin to repay their loans. He instructed two of his design engineers to begin secret work on a new car, the Bricklin Chairman, a black luxury vehicle that would sell for $25,000. At the same time, Bricklin's U.S. companies stopped forwarding payments for cars shipped from New Brunswick. In July and August, nearly $4 million (wholesale price) worth of cars were shipped to the U.S. without payment. And while Bricklin was carrying on these contortions, while making assurances that his New Brunswick company was making a profit, the New Brunswick government began to receive reports that would persuade it, finally, to put Bricklin in receivership.

Bricklin had begun his public relations campaign in Fredericton in April, when he told a group of businessmen that the Bricklin companies would be making a profit within a month. At that time, he had urged the New Brunswick Liberals to "bury the political hatchet" and leave his companies alone. In the weeks following the Fredericton speech, Bricklin and other company officials made a series of speeches in New Brunswick to the effect that production hurdles had been overcome and the Bricklin companies were beginning to make a profit. Hatfield contributed to the campaign by making frequent appearances with the Bricklin car, including a well-publicized appearance at the Ontario Science Centre in Toronto, where the province of New Brunswick had placed a Bricklin on exhibit.

In June and July, the public relations efforts continued. On June 18, a week after the New Brunswick legislature adjourned its spring sitting, Leon Klein, the former Montreal promoter who now held the position of vice-president of administration and finance with General Vehicle Inc., told a service club in Campbellton that Bricklin was making a cash profit. Klein bragged that he had been the man to introduce Malcolm Bricklin to New Brunswick. "I've been with it from the beginning," he said. Klein said he would take a certain pleasure in telling the "doubting Thomases" about Bricklin's success. For some of the skeptics, particularly those in the press, he said, it would be more a question of "throwing it in their faces." Klein was never very good at public relations.

On June 20, Malcolm Bricklin told a meeting of chartered accountants in St. Andrews, in southern New Brunswick, that he would not have to borrow any more money from the New Brunswick government. He was making a cash profit. Bricklin said his car was bringing rewards to New Brunswick. "Today we have a car with which you can go anywhere in the world," he said, "and which will be recognized and associated with New Brunswick."

The public relations campaign began to have an effect. In late June, the Canadian Press noted in a story that the "unannounced" campaign, combined with reports that production had risen to about 20 cars a day at Saint John, seemed to have stilled criticism of Bricklin. "Critical newspaper editorials that used to come at the rate of two or three a week have largely disappeared in the past few weeks," the story said. "Equally important, the Liberal Opposition's extensive criticism of the project — particularly the government's $20 million investment in it — has died down as well."

Virtually the only skeptical voice in the summer of 1975 belonged to Charlie Russell, a disk jockey on CJCJ in the Carleton County town of Woodstock, and his was a jovial skepticism. "O' the Bricklin, O' the Bricklin," sang Russell, on a record that would sell 5,000 copies within six months, "Is it just another Edsel, wait and see." Russell would later present a copy of his record to Hatfield, while thanking him for "having launched the car that launched my career."

It was a false spring. Almost certainly the public relations campaign was intended as much to cajole the New Brunswick government, whose consultants were delving into the Bricklin project, as it was to calm the suspicions of New Brunswick's citizens. Between speeches, Bricklin and Klein and others were meeting almost continuously in Bricklin's lavish Scottsdale think tank. Bricklin was running out of money again. According to public statements by Klein, the $7.5 million loan provided by the province in monthly segments since January had been spent by June. The loan had been intended to give Bricklin the large block of operating capital necessary to overcome day-to-day money worries and to move onto a surer footing. But, as with earlier loans, much of the money had been used to pay pressing debts. The rest was quickly swallowed by the inefficient Bricklin organization. Production problems had not been overcome, as the government's consultants would discover in the summer of 1975. As many as 25 per cent of the parts produced at Minto had to be thrown away because of poor bonding and breakage. More parts were wasted at Saint John. The wastage went demonstrably higher as Bricklin personnel struggled in the spring and summer months to raise production. Klein's assertions that Bricklin was now generating enough money on its own to stay in operation were ludicrous, as the government's consultants would discover.

Bricklin's think tank had other problems to contend with. By the summer of 1975, the U.S. dealer network was in a state of collapse. The government had consistently defended its loans to Bricklin on grounds that the Bricklin car had won clear market acceptance, and that car production had been pre-sold for years. By the summer of 1975, this was no longer so. Dealer resistance to the car and to the entire Bricklin marketing setup was growing. The long-standing problems were still apparent. Dealers had paid franchise fees, but had not received cars. They had paid for parts and tools and had not received them. Now there was a new problem. Dealers who received cars, often after two years of waiting, were outraged by the poor quality. By June, 1975, Bricklin had shipped about 1,800 cars, and most of the dealers who received them were up in arms. The gull-wing doors leaked. Often, the doors wouldn't open. The windows leaked. Dealers had to advise buyers not to drive their cars in the rain. In many cases, the interior fitting of the car was terrible. The wiring was often faulty. Between the faulty wiring and the sticking doors, Bricklin's safety vehicle was a fire hazard. The dealers sought warranty for repairs, and couldn't get it. They couldn't get repair parts either, or trained Bricklin servicemen, or even service advice, all of which had been promised, and, in some cases, paid for. Bricklin's U.S. companies had been set up to sell franchises and advertising kits, which is what Bricklin knew how to do. They had not been set up to provide service for cars. In this respect, they were no different than any of Bricklin's earlier sales efforts. He had sold franchises for motor scooters, but had not delivered the parts and service he had promised. He had sold Subaru franchises and cars, but had not delivered service or parts. He sold Bricklin cars, and then left the dealers in the cold when customers complained about the poor quality of the cars. On August 20, 1975, Bricklin would write to the dealers, in response to the developing barrage of complaints, that they ought to provide service to Bricklin owners consistent with their standards of service in relation to the other types of cars they sold. His letter wouldn't refer to his earlier promises of parts, trained servicemen and full warrantees. But by August, Bricklin's reputation would have spread completely among the U.S. dealers. He couldn't sell another franchise.

The production problems remained unsolved. Bricklin was out of money. The dealership network was collapsing. In early July, 1975, Bricklin's U.S. sales companies stopped returning payments to New Brunswick for cars shipped from Saint John to the U.S. The practice would continue until August 18, when Garvie, the province's economic growth minister, would learn of it and order a halt to car shipments. By that time, according to government and company sources, 500 cars would have been shipped from Saint John without payment. The total owed to the New Brunswick company for the cars would be $3.6 million. The cars, in turn, would be sold to Bricklin dealers at a marked-up price.

By the summer of 1975, under Garvie's direction, the government had managed to establish a reporting system of sorts between the Bricklin companies and itself. The system wasn't completely reliable because the accountants and consultants appointed in December and January were simply unable to obtain the information needed for accurate reports. Nonetheless, they began to make disquieting reports to the government in the early summer of 1975. The reports would continue throughout the summer.

Touche, Ross and Co. Ltd., a nationally-known firm of accountants, had been hired to audit the books of Bricklin Canada Ltd. when the government announced new financing to Bricklin in December. The Bricklin accounts had never been audited. They never would be. Throughout the first half of 1975, a Touche, Ross auditor worked full-time, with occasional part-time assistance, on an audit of the Bricklin books. It was an impossible job. Entries had not been made. Bills could not be tracked down. The Bricklin books were in complete confusion. Many bills had been simply thrown into files and boxes. No record had been made of them. Eventually, Touche, Ross reported to the government that it could not perform an unqualified audit of the Bricklin books.

Sawyer and Campbell, two Wespac consultants with automotive experience, had begun in January to look over Bricklin's operations in New Brunswick and in the U.S. Gradually, they had established long-range goals for the Bricklin project. They wanted clear lines of management, and controls on production expenses. They could not obtain complete figures, but it was apparent that production costs were running over $13,000 per car, and that the costs were not being brought down. Each month there were heavy losses. The production problems were continuing. Bricklin had reached a production rate of twenty-four cars per day for a brief period in April, but production was quickly cut back to sixteen cars per day as car quality problems became apparent.

The reports of the Wespac consultants were confirmed by reports filed by Clarkson Gordon and Company Ltd., which had been monitoring car transfer prices and production expenses throughout the spring. On the basis of advice from Clarkson Gordon, Garvie had increased the transfer price for cars by nearly $2,000 in April. In the summer months, Clarkson Gordon continued to report that production costs were running far above the selling price of the Bricklin car.

In July, under pressure from the government, Bricklin asked Clarkson Gordon to prepare a detailed operating budget for the Bricklin companies for the next fiscal year. Clarkson Gordon received assurances from the government that it would be paid for its work, and then began to develop a budget. Meetings were held with Klein, who had developed some projections for the U.S. companies. A Clarkson Gordon accountant was installed at Minto on a full-time basis in an effort to analyze the cost of body parts production. The Clarkson Gordon officials would work twelve to fourteen hours a day in the next six weeks in an attempt to put together a budget for the Bricklin companies. In the later weeks, they would be under increasing pressure to finish the budget. With Bricklin's enormous financial problems becoming apparent in the late summer of 1975, the Clarkson Gordon budget would become the key to Bricklin's future.

In June, Garvie had sent Wheatley, the young economic growth employee who had been assigned to the Bricklin project, to the U.S. to assess the condition of Bricklin's sales operations. Wheatley returned with a dismal report. The operation was collapsing.

On July 26, Bricklin attended the annual Bricklin Canada Ltd. directors' meeting in Saint John. Avery was with him. Bricklin was in summer clothes. He wore a shirt with little faces of Marilyn Monroe on it. "We're gonna make it," Bricklin told a reporter. The Bricklin project would need no more money from the New Brunswick government. "From now on, when we need money we can raise it through the normal financial channels."

After the directors' meeting, Garvie summoned Bricklin and Henry to a meeting at the Centennial Building in Fredericton. Nason, the deputy economic growth minister, also attended. Garvie instructed Bricklin and Henry to implement changes suggested by the Wespac consultants. Bricklin and Henry were told to make changes in management policy. They were told to provide the government with firm operating budgets, tied to car sales. They were told to prepare cash flow budgets. They were to prepare production projections, and to establish cost projections that were realistic. Bricklin agreed wholeheartedly. He would do all of that, and more.

In early August, Bricklin organized a meeting of Bricklin officials at the Hyatt House in Toronto. The government was not informed of the meeting. Henry attended. So did Avery, Bricklin's lifestyle adviser, and Leon Klein, who had become comptroller of Bricklin's U.S. companies. So did Albert Bricklin, and Scully, the comptroller of Bricklin Canada Ltd. Bricklin had problems. What would they do about the government's pressure tactics? Where would they get more money? Klein had prepared some projections showing that Bricklin needed another $10 million in a hurry. Malcolm Bricklin ventured his guess that Garvie would come up with the $10 million. If not, they were in trouble. Albert Bricklin exploded. Malcolm had not looked after the family interests, he said. Malcolm had made bad decisions. The Bricklins were losing control of their own company. Albert announced that he was resigning. He was through. No one took him seriously. When Klein prepared the Bricklin companies' proposed budgets shortly afterwards, Albert was still on the payroll, at a salary of $60,000.

In mid-August, while Klein was preparing his budgets, which were intended partly to form the basis of a new request to New Brunswick for money, Garvie was informed by the government's consultants in Saint John that money wasn't being returned to New Brunswick for car shipments. Garvie quickly summoned Henry to Fredericton. At the same time, he halted a shipment of cars that was loaded and ready to leave Saint John. When Henry arrived, Garvie told him that no more cars would be shipped to the U.S. until payments were brought up to date. Henry objected, without success. Henry left Garvie's office and called Bricklin, who was in Scottsdale. Bricklin quickly made a telephone call to Garvie and began to argue, but Garvie was adamant. No more cars would be shipped. Garvie was now waiting for the Clarkson Gordon budget report.

Officers of the Clarkson Gordon Company had traveled to the U.S. in July to view Bricklin's American operations. They had met with Klein and had received copies of Klein's operating expense projections for the coming year. The Clarkson officers realized immediately that Klein's projections would result in further vast losses in the coming year. They began to pare down Klein's projections. On September 9, they met with the board of directors of Bricklin Canada Ltd., including Bricklin who was chairman of the board, and discussed Klein's budget proposals. The Klein-Bricklin budget forecast immediate new money needs of $10 million, which Bricklin hoped the New Brunswick government would provide.

After the directors' meeting, the Clarkson officers began once more to pare the Klein projections. They were under pressure. Bricklin's money needs were urgent. The government was waiting anxiously for the Clarkson report. It would determine the future of the Bricklin project.

On September 15, while the government was still waiting for Clarkson to report, Hatfield announced that new financing of $1.2 million, in the form of letters of credit at the Bank of Montreal, would be advanced to Bricklin. Hatfield said in a prepared statement the money was required "to assure the supply of drive train components" at Saint John. In fact, the money was needed to meet the payrolls at Saint John and Minto and to hold off Bricklin's creditors while the government waited for the Clarkson report. Bricklin had begun to bounce cheques again. For example, a $60,000 cheque paid to Plastics Maritimes Ltd., the major supplier of fibreglass to Bricklin, had just come bouncing back. So had another cheque for $75,000 to the same company. Word had begun to circulate among Bricklin suppliers that the car company was going under, and the suppliers were making moves to protect themselves. The government hoped to stabilize the situation with its new financing.

"This additional provincial support," said Hatfield's statement, distributed by the New Brunswick Information Service, "is required because of additional erosion of working capital resulting from continuing start-up problems." His statement ended with an optimistic note. "To date, Bricklin Canada Ltd. has produced in excess of 2,700 of its gull-wing sports styled safety automobiles. Daily production is being maintained in the 20-40 vehicles per day range. Employment at the Saint John plant is now 500 and 200 are employed in Minto, New Brunswick."

Three days after Hatfield made his announcement of new financing, Bricklin Canada Ltd. laid off 250 workers at Saint John. The company said the layoffs would last until a changeover was made in tooling for Bricklin's 1976 models.

Hatfield's announcement and the layoffs fueled speculation. Rumors quickly spread that Bricklin was going under. Government and company officials were chased for comments, but they maintained a tight-lipped silence. On Friday, September 20, Garvie was cornered by a reporter at a meeting in St. Andrews, where Bricklin had asserted three months earlier that he would need no more money from the government. Garvie told the reporter the government was "not nearly as optimistic" about the Bricklin project as it had been a few months earlier. "When you have to be putting money in continually, you lose some of your optimism," he said.

Speculation was rampant over the weekend. Officials could not be reached for comment, which only added to the rumors. On Monday, September 23, Henry was reached for a reaction. "I had no knowledge he (Garvie) had such thoughts on his mind," said Henry. "I'm convinced more than ever that Bricklin is more viable today than it's ever been. There should be more enthusiasm, not less."

On the same day, Hatfield was questioned in Saint John, where he was attending a meeting of the Saint John-Fundy Progressive Conservative Association. Hatfield said the government was re-appraising the Bricklin project, but that he and his cabinet, including Garvie, "are still enthusiastic about this project, but concerned about the present economic situation." Garvie, meanwhile, wasn't answering his phone.

On September 23, the Bricklin Canada Ltd. board of directors held a special meeting at the Keddy Motor Inn at Saint John to discuss Bricklin's budget, which had just been completed by Clarkson. Reporters quickly discovered the meeting and stationed themselves in the motor inn. The Saint John reporters had learned long ago to detect a Bricklin meeting whenever they saw a group of Bricklin cars in one place.

The board meeting began at 10 o'clock in the morning. When Bricklin emerged at noon, he refused to answer questions. "I'm sorry, but it's no comment," he said, "I've been sworn to secrecy." Late in the afternoon, the meeting broke up. Bricklin again refused to comment. He said the board meeting would continue the next morning at Keddy's.

Chapter 16

THE LATE BRICKLIN BUDGET

On September 23, Garvie received a copy of budget projections prepared by Clarkson Gordon for Bricklin Canada Ltd. and for General Vehicle Inc. and its U.S. subsidiary companies. The projections were for the fiscal year ending June 30, 1976. Copies had been forwarded to the directors of Bricklin Canada Ltd., who were meeting in Saint John. The Clarkson Gordon projections represented the first substantial budget prepared for the Bricklin companies since they went into operation in New Brunswick in 1973. But even these projections could not be wholly accurate. They were built on company financial statements that had not been audited. Accountants for Touche Ross & Co. were still attempting to sort the bills for the fiscal year ending June 30, 1975. Much of the data in the Clarkson projections was supplied by Klein, Bricklin's accountant. Many of the projections, including those related to car body costs at Minto, were little more than guesswork.

The company budgets were prefaced with unaudited financial statements for the fiscal year ending June 30, 1975. According to Bricklin company sources, several loss figures in the statements were understated because all company bills had not been entered, or even sorted, when the statements were prepared. Even so, the losses in Bricklin's first year of operation were enormous. Bricklin Canada Ltd. showed accumulated losses of $16.64 million at June 30, 1975. General Vehicle Inc. showed accumulated losses of $6 million.

The financial statement for Bricklin Canada Ltd. listed several nebulous assets. A figure of $1 million was listed for development rights to the Bricklin car (the figure had been agreed upon by the government and Bricklin in 1973, and was written into the June, 1973 agreement). A figure of $1.77 million was listed for cash collateral accounts, which included $1 million deposited in a non-interest-bearing account with the First Pennsylvania Bank. A figure of $6.56 million was listed for investment in equipment and tooling, but this included the temporary Minto tooling which would have to be replaced within months. Other assets included inventories of $5.2 million and an amount of $894,000 owed to Bricklin Canada Ltd. by General Vehicle Inc. for 124 cars that had been shipped to the U.S., but not paid for. The liabilities of Bricklin Canada Ltd. included current accounts payable of $6.7 million (including $4.6 million owed to suppliers, which was almost certainly understated), current debt payments of $2.3 million and long-term debts of $20.1 million, owed to the province of New Brunswick.

The financial statement for General Vehicle Inc. was full of curiosities. The company's assets included "pre-operating expenses" of $2.5 million, of which $2 million had been loaned by the First Pennsylvania Bank. The $2 million loan was Malcolm Bricklin's investment in his car companies. The assets of General Vehicle also included an investment of $806,000 in Bricklin's Phoenix raceway, including the land and furniture and equipment. The liabilities of General Vehicle Inc. at June 30, 1975 included a bank overdraft of $226,300, a long-term debt of $2.6 million, an amount of $1.3 million owed on Bricklin dealer kits, and an amount of $894,000 owed to Bricklin Canada Ltd. for cars. According to the statement, General Vehicle owed monthly interest payments of nearly $25,000 on its debts, of which $16,000 was payable to the First Pennsylvania Bank, and $7,300 to FasTrack International Inc., which was the company's own raceway.

The total share equity investment in General Vehicle Inc. was listed at $72,700, of which $20,000 had been contributed by the New Brunswick government for two million, or one-quarter, of the GVI shares. Assertions by New Brunswick government spokesmen that General Vehicle Inc. had $14.1 million invested in the Bricklin car before New Brunswick became involved were ludicrous.

In its projections for the 1975-1976 fiscal year, Clarkson Gordon reported that Bricklin Canada Ltd. would continue to sustain heavy losses, even if the company was able to make extensive reductions in production costs. By March 31, 1976, the operating losses of Bricklin Canada Ltd. would rise to an estimated $20.7 million. In the same period, the company would be unable to make any payments on its long-term debts to the province. Clarkson Gordon projected that General Vehicle Inc. would make a profit of $1.4 million in the 1975-1976 fiscal year if it carried out widespread cost reductions, including the closure of its Scottsdale and Whippany offices, restrictions on Malcolm Bricklin's flying expenses, and salary reductions. But, even with this profit, General Vehicle would be unable to meet loans that would come due during the year. If these projections were correct — and they were a minimum — Bricklin would need new capital of $10 million. In late August, Bricklin had asked the government for that amount.

The projected scale of operations for Bricklin Canada Ltd. was far below the scale that Bricklin had envisaged. Clarkson Gordon projected that the Saint John plant would build 6,269 cars in the year ending June 30, 1976, or about one-half the number that Bricklin had dreamed of building. The projected transfer price for the cars (the price at which they would be sold to General Vehicle Inc.) was $7,400 each, but it was a long gamble that the cost of building cars could be pulled down to that level. Clarkson Gordon listed the production cost per car at $8,973 in July, 1975, but this could be only an estimate. There were, for example, no reliable figures for body parts production at Minto. Clarkson Gordon projected that the July production cost would be pulled down to $7,401 per car by October, 1975, and to $7,199 by December, but this projection could be little more than informed speculation. It assumed, for example, that the 25 per cent rate of parts loss through scrap at Minto in June, 1975, could be reduced to 10 per cent by December. Since the scrap rate at Minto had increased in the spring and summer of 1975 as Bricklin struggled to raise production, the assumption was not a valid one.

Clarkson Gordon took fewer chances with its projections in regard to another production problem — that of the gull-wing doors. An amount of $400 per car was budgeted to pay for warranty claims on cars equipped with hydraulic doors, and $150 per car was budgeted for Bricklins which were to be equipped with screw-type doors — the mechanism had not been perfected. It was anticipated that most owners of cars with hydraulic doors would seek a change-over. Two-thirds of the warranty budget was assigned to Bricklin Canada Ltd. in simple recognition of the fact that General Vehicle had long ago established the practice of passing on warranty claims to the New Brunwick company, although cars were sold to dealers by Bricklin's U.S. companies.

In another section of the proposed budget for Bricklin Canada Ltd., Clarkson Gordon recognized a further longstanding practice — that of billings by General Vehicle Inc. to the New Brunswick company for research, development, engineering and car testing costs. (Clarkson Gordon would attempt to reduce GVI charges to the New Brunswick company in these four areas to $1,089,092 during the budget year). Bricklin Canada Ltd. paid the cost of developing the Bricklin car. In the 1975-1976 budget, it would pay the cost of another Bricklin brainstorm. Bricklin had assigned Herb Grasse and Richard Vollmer, two of his design engineers, to develop a new car that would be called the Bricklin Chairman. Grasse's salary was $24,996, paid by Bricklin Canada Ltd. Vollmer's salary was $39,996, paid by Bricklin Canada Ltd. At the time of the Clarkson Gordon budget, the two men were already at work on the car. It would be bigger than the standard Bricklin. It would be black. It would have a Continental engine and gold-plated fixtures. The buyer of a Bricklin Chairman would be flown by private jet to Saint John to watch his car being produced. The car would be delivered to his home. It would cost $25,000. It was at this point that Bricklin began to describe to close associates the future of the Bricklin organization. He intended to buy the Empire State Building and use it as his world headquarters. Every hour, every day, somewhere in the world, a jet aircraft would be flying on some mission connected with the Bricklin organization. Bricklin's dreams were getting out of hand.

In an effort to reduce losses, Clarkson Gordon attempted to bat some of the frills out of the Bricklin Canada Ltd. operation. By October, 1975, the company practice of leasing cars on behalf of its executives would end. The New Brunswick company was leasing nine cars, at a cost of $250 each per month, for its executives to drive. Clarkson Gordon also reduced the travel budget of Bricklin Canada Ltd. executives from $27,400, which was spent in June, to a standard $4,000 per month. The travel budget covered nine people, including Ralph Henry. "Considering the duties (they) have to perform, it was estimated that $4,000 per month should be sufficient," said the budget note. In a miscellaneous account, Clarkson Gordon noted that the New Brunswick company was paying rent of $600 a month to house Henry in Saint John. Clarkson Gordon also budgeted for a decrease in long distance telephone calls, from $12,700 spent in June to a standard $8,000 per month. Clarkson Gordon budgeted a total of $182,400 for professional services for Bricklin Canada Ltd. during the year, including $100,000 for Clarkson Gordon. The accounting firm was aware that Bricklin might not have the money to pay its fee, and had received assurances that it would be paid by the New Brunswick government before it agreed to prepare the budget. An amount of $30,000 was budgeted for the Touche Ross accountants who were still sorting the Bricklin bills.

In a section dealing with loans, Clarkson Gordon budgeted for interest payments by Bricklin Canada Ltd. of $203,900 per month in the period from July, 1975, to January, 1976, and $215,400 per month in the period from February, 1976, to June. Interest payments for the year would total $2.5 million. The payments were for loans from the province of New Brunswick, the Bank of Montreal and the First Pennsylvania Bank. A further $4,000 per month was budgeted to pay for interest on overdrafts at the Bank of Montreal. However, there was no amount in the budget to make payments on the principle amount of the loans. Bricklin Canada Ltd. couldn't afford to pay any of its loans.

The budget for operations at Minto, where Bricklin body parts were produced, contained much less detail. The fibreglass-acrylic body was intended to enable the production of an inexpensive car, but tooling, bonding and scrap problems had driven Minto costs towards the heavens. Nobody had accurate data on production costs at Minto.

"The preparation of the Minto budget was made much more difficult owing to the lack of past actual cost data from which to project forward," Clarkson Gordon wrote in an introduction to the Minto budget. Some figures for the past four months of operation at Minto had been provided, but these were "in most cases inaccurate," the accountants wrote. "It was not deemed necessary to correct this data, for this would have involved a review of all supplier invoices and an analysis of all material requisitions." Clarkson Gordon didn't have time for such a review, because it was under pressure to get a budget to the government. The "inaccurate" Minto costs figured, of course, in the cost of car production, which in turn was supposed to determine the car transfer price to the U.S.

The proposed operating budget for General Vehicle Inc. and its subsidiary companies was bulkier. The Clarkson Gordon accountants had traveled to the U.S. and viewed Bricklin's American operations, and they were prepared to cut them down with a vengeance. The GVI budget, with Brickin's acquiescence, provided for the phasing out of Bricklin offices in Scottsdale and the parts centre that had been established at Whippany, New Jersey. There was also a general proposal to "work with the company's management to develop an adequate level of controls." In other words, Bricklin had not developed a system of accounting controls during the period he was receiving New Brunswick funds. Even in September, 1975, there were not controls over such items as inter-company transfers and billings between Bricklin's U.S. companies and the New Brunswick company.

The General Vehicle Inc. budget was prefaced with a revealing set of comparative statistics. The margin of profit or loss to Bricklin Canada Ltd. was compared with that of General Vehicle Inc. on the sale of 396 Bricklin cars in July, 1975. The New Brunswick company lost a recorded $1,813 on each car sold to the U.S. company, for a percentage of loss on sales of 24.1 per cent. On the same cars, which General Vehicle Inc. sold to dealers for $9,388, the U.S. company made a net profit of $184 per car. Clarkson Gordon projected that by November, 1975, the loss per car to Bricklin Canada Ltd. would be reduced to $1,145. General Vehicle Inc.'s profit per car was projected to rise to $404.

While it was profiting from the sales of New Brunswick-built cars, Bricklin's U.S. operation was continuing to bill the New Brunswick company for a host of charges, including the salaries of U.S. employees. According to the Clarkson Gordon budget, Bricklin Canada Ltd. was paying 80 per cent of the General Vehicle Inc. salaries. In July, 1975, Bricklin Canada Ltd. would be billed for U.S. salaries totaling $74,311. General Vehicle would pay salaries of $18,578 the same month. Payments by the New Brunswick companies for the U.S. salaries would decrease during the year with the phasing out of the Whippany and Scottsdale offices, and with a reduction in the number of employees at the Livonia plant from 70 to 40. By December, the New Brunswick company would be paying U.S. salaries of only $49,962 a month. For the budget year, the New Brunswick company would pay total U.S. salaries of $667,879. General Vehicle Inc. would pay salaries of $166,971.

A number of Bricklins and close associates were receiving substantial salaries. Malcolm Bricklin was drawing a basic salary of $120,000, exclusive of travel and related costs. Albert Bricklin, who by September was in charge of the Phoenix speedway and, of all things, cost reduction, was drawing $60,000. Gertrude Bricklin, Malcolm's mother, was drawing $30,000. She was a vice-president. Clarkson Gordon would knock $1,000 per month off her salary. Barbara Jonas, Malcolm's sister, was drawing $37,000. She was a vice-president. Clarkson Gordon would phase her out. Ben Bricklin, Malcolm's uncle, was drawing a paltry $18,000. His position was "new dealership development" (At this point, there wasn't a dealer who would touch Bricklin). Michael Avery, Bricklin's mentor, was drawing $24,000 as "assistant to the chairman," but was slated to become the president of Bricklin Vehicle Corporation at a salary of $90,000. Pat Carfagno, Bricklin's personal secretary for years, was drawing $23,600. Colleen McCabe, whom Bricklin would soon marry, had just climbed onto the payroll.

The Clarkson Gordon accountants attempted to reduce some of Bricklin's promotion-related and joy-related expenses. The travel budgets of GVI executives would be reduced from an average of nearly $40,000 a month to about $4,000 by November, 1975. The use of a jet airplane would end. So would such miscellaneous items as "drawings" by Malcolm Bricklin of $25,252 from GVI business expenses, in addition to his salary. A chauffeur would be removed from the GVI payroll. The GVI public relations department, including Barbara Jonas, would be removed from the payroll in November.

After cutting and paring the Bricklin budgets as much as possible, Clarkson Gordon prepared a budget critique. This was forwarded to Bricklin in a September 23 letter accompanying the projections for General Vehicle Inc. Copies of the critique were sent to the government. Clarkson Gordon said in its critique it doubted that Bricklin's current management was capable of remaining within the budget projections. In other words, the operating losses projected for the coming year were a minimum. Under Bricklin's management, they could go much higher. The $10 million requested by Bricklin might, like his earlier requests, turn out to be not enough.

The Clarkson Gordon letter listed four "critical assumptions" that it said could upset the budget projections. One was management. "The budget for Bricklin Canada Ltd. included a significant reduction in the material cost per vehicle," said the letter. "The personnel included in the General Vehicle Inc. budget are responsible for most of the work required to achieve the planned savings. We are not certain that the resources, as budgeted, can achieve the savings." In other words, Clarkson Gordon didn't believe the present management could make the cost reductions. The other three critical assumptions listed by Clarkson Gordon were market acceptance of the Bricklin car (Clarkson Gordon was aware of the problems in Bricklin's dealership organization), financing, and car quality (the poor quality of Bricklin cars produced to that time had created a dealer and consumer backlash).

"In total," said the Clarkson Gordon critique, "our impression is that the budget was not prepared against a set of company needs, such as the four critical requirements (the critical assumptions) set out on pages 2 to 4 of our letter of September 8, 1975 (a letter to Bricklin in which Clarkson Gordon had registered its initial criticisms of Klein's projections). "We suggest that a more precise statement of company goals over the next twelve months is required before the attached budget is given to management as the operating plan."

The goals that Clarkson Gordon felt should be provided for in the operating plan included (1) Correction of problems within the vehicle which created dealer resistence, (2) Correction of problems with the vehicle which created major warranty costs, (3) Rehabilitation of the current dealer network, which was collapsing, (4) Reduction of the bill of material cost — Clarkson Gordon realized that cost reductions contained in its budget projections were not a certainty, but were largely a hope, (5) Development of the California market.

In a concluding section of its critique, Clarkson Gordon noted that it had prepared the budget projections on the basis of information provided by Bricklin management. The projections relating to U.S. operations were provided primarily by Klein. Clarkson Gordon also noted that it had proposed to Bricklin's management on September 12 that an adequate level of budget controls be implemented. "The proposal has been accepted and we are now in the process of developing them." More than two years after the New Brunswick government began to finance Bricklin, there were no adequate budget controls in place, despite government hopes and despite government public statements that its string of consultants and accountants would regulate Bricklin's spending.

Garvie received the Clarkson Gordon projections on September 23. He saw the forecasts of further heavy losses, which would result even if widespread reductions were made in production costs. Bricklin had already asked for $10 million. According to Clarkson Gordon, even this amount might not be enough. There was no end in sight to the amount of money the government would have to put into Bricklin. Garvie read the Clarkson Gordon expressions of doubt about the management ability of Bricklin and his personnel. Garvie had no choice. He decided to shut down Bricklin Canada Ltd.

Chapter 17

RECEIVERSHIP

On Wednesday, September 24, Garvie checked into his sixth-floor office in the Centennial Building and then took the elevator to the second floor for the weekly meeting of the Conservative cabinet. Garvie had discussed his decision with Hatfield. Nason, the deputy economic growth minister, had been informed. So had the Bank of Montreal, the First Pennsylvania Bank, Clarkson Gordon, and the two Wespac consultants. They would attend the receivership proceedings. Garvie made his recommendation to the cabinet to place Bricklin Canada Ltd. in receivership. The cabinet supported the economic growth minister.

Hatfield and Garvie left the cabinet meeting and flew by chartered helicopter to Saint John to attend the board of directors' meeting, which was in its second day. They landed outside the city to avoid reporters, and were driven to the Holiday Inn. By pre-arrangement, the directors' meeting had been switched at the last moment from Keddy's to the Holiday Inn in another effort to fool reporters. Hatfield and Garvie went to a room that had been reserved for them, and conferred. They prepared to go downstairs to the directors' meeting. An aide informed them that reporters had located the meeting, and were in the hallway downstairs. Hatfield and Garvie sneaked down a set of back-stairs and into the kitchen of the Holiday Inn. They went through a kitchen service entry and into a salon adjacent to the meeting room, hoping to avoid the reporters, but ran into a group that had gathered in the salon. Hatfield and Garvie walked through a flurry of questions into the directors' meeting.

Inside, after the formality of greetings, Garvie said that the New Brunswick government would put no more money into Bricklin Canada Ltd. There was a moment of silence. A Bank of Montreal representative left the room to tell his bank to stop accepting Bricklin cheques. Bricklin conferred with his legal advisers and then made a motion to put Bricklin Canada Ltd. in receivership. For a moment, there was utter silence. Then there was some sporadic conversation about what would happen next. Then the directors' meeting broke up. It was 3:45 p.m. Reporters surrounded the Bricklin and government officials as they left the room. There were terse refusals to comment. Hatfield told reporters the directors' meeting had been adjourned to an unspecified time and location.

Hatfield, Garvie and Bricklin left the motor inn together. Outside, Hatfield shook hands with several officials, including Bricklin. The men climbed into cars and went their separate ways. Malcolm Bricklin got into a Bricklin car and drove off into his own personal sunset. Ralph Henry, who had attended the directors' meeting, went home and began to prepare for a vacation. He would leave for the Caymen Islands. He would be unreachable. Several months later, he would emerge as a Philadelphia-based consultant.

On September 25, the receivership proceedings were begun in the New Brunswick Supreme Court in Fredericton. At the same time, the First Pennsylvania Bank began court proceedings to take control of the Bricklin assets in New Brunswick. Shortly after five o'clock in the afternoon, the New Brunswick Information Service carried a short announcement by Hatfield that Bricklin had been placed in receivership. The statement said that Bricklin's secured creditors, which included the government, the Bank of Montreal and the First Pennsylvania Bank, had decided in meetings over the past two weeks that they couldn't provide further financing. Hatfield was not available for comment. He was attending a meeting of premiers in Quebec City.

On Friday, September 26, at a brief Supreme Court hearing in Fredericton, the Clarkson Company Ltd., a division of Clarkson Gordon & Company specializing in bankruptcies and receiverships, was appointed receiver of Bricklin Canada Ltd.

The same day, Hatfield returned to Fredericton from Quebec City and scheduled a press conference for five o'clock in the afternoon. During the day he met with party supporters who had arrived in Fredericton for the annual meeting of the New Brunswick Progressive Conservative Party. The party's election of officers and routine vote of confidence in its leader, Hatfield, would take place the following day, which was Saturday.

Room G-12, the large first-floor conference room in the Centennial Building where the government holds many of its press conferences, was packed at five o'clock. Besides reporters and several camera crews, members of Hatfield's cabinet and civil servants had crowded into seats. Hatfield, flanked by Garvie, began with a brief statement in which he said he would describe circumstances leading to the receivership decision. He said that new financing of $7.5 million provided to Bricklin in January, combined with management changes, seemed to make it possible that Bricklin would achieve a "positive financial result" in 1975. "By April," he said, "the prospects had improved even further. Some consolidation in the management and facilities had been realized (he didn't describe these), and more importantly, production had increased significantly. Our analysis in May gave reason for cautious optimism about the project."

Despite the "real but marginal improvement" that occurred in the spring, production costs and "general economic conditions" continued to erode Bricklin's financial position, Hatfield said. In August, he said, the government instructed Bricklin to prepare a realistic operating plan by September 8 and to raise outside capital. Bricklin did neither, he said. Instead, Bricklin presented the government with projections in September that would require "considerable" amounts of short-term financing and "substantial" long-term financing. The money would have to come from the government.

"Although the government had always believed that the potential advantages of the project were worth the financial risk taken," Hatfield said, "we have also known from the beginning that there was a point beyond which the government should not, on its own, risk additional government funds on this one project. That point has been reached . . . "

Hatfield went on to say the government still had confidence in the Bricklin car. It would explore "every reasonable opportunity" to find a buyer or operator for the Bricklin plants. In the meantime, it would guarantee the payroll for employees at Saint John and Minto for the week just ended — an expenditure of $200,000.

Hatfield said the government wouldn't allow the Bricklin collapse to hamper its ongoing development efforts. "It is more important than ever to devote ourselves to economic growth and job creation in our province, and this remains the top priority of our government." In this connection, he had decided to carry out an earlier commitment to leave for Japan on the weekend, to meet with government and industry officials. He would ask them if they were interested in Bricklin. "I regard this initiative as an important step in our ongoing efforts to attract investment and development to New Brunswick," Hatfield said. He would be back in two weeks.

In response to a flurry of reporters' questions that followed his prepared statement, Hatfield said little. He declined to answer most questions on grounds that he didn't want to interfere with the work of the Bricklin receiver. Had he begun discussions with anyone in New Brunswick to take over the Bricklin companies? (One rumor in the wake of the receivership announcement was that the K.C. Irving interests in Saint John would take over the Bricklin plants. The Irvings quickly denied the rumor. The Irvings did have one connection with Bricklin. Irving Oil Ltd. had purchased three Bricklin cars from Bricklin Vehicle Corporation, to be used in the promotion of Irving oil products. The cars were paid for with cash, although Bricklin Canada Ltd. owed Irving a rumored $73,000. After Bricklin was placed in receivership, the Irvings stored their cars away as an investment). Hatfield said he would have to wait for a report from the receiver. Would he resign? No. Eventually the press conference adjourned.

The same day, Bricklin issued a press release from his Scottsdale think tank, to which he and Avery had withdrawn to console one another. Copies of the release were distributed to Bricklin dealers, who were alarmed by the New Brunswick receivership announcement. Most of the dealers were owed cars, parts, service or money by Bricklin. Bricklin's press release, written on a Bricklin Vehicle Corporation letterhead, was inventive. "Lack of agreement between the principle lenders of Bricklin Canada Ltd. (BCL), manufacturers of the Bricklin SV1 sports car, caused a temporary shutdown of the firm's assembly plants at New Brunswick, Canada, Sept. 25," said the release.

"The province of New Brunswick and the First Pennsylvania Bank held discussions for two weeks to decide who would provide the $10 million capital necessary for expansion, inventory and normal business functions.

"The two lenders were unable to agree on the method of implementing the loan.

"We have received literally thousands of telephone calls from people who shared our dream, wanting to help in any way possible during this present crisis," said Bricklin in his press release. "Even children, whose identification with the Bricklin was so strong, they offered their allowances to insure there would be a Bricklin when they got old enough to drive." For them and for his workers, Bricklin said he would strive to re-open "communications" with the province so the Bricklin project could succeed. Then Bricklin and Avery got ready to repair to the University of Nebraska in Lincoln, Neb., where, the following week, Bricklin would attend a "weekend-in-residence" for businessmen, sponsored by the university.

On September 27, the day after his press conference, Hatfield attended the annual meeting of the provincial Progressive Conservative party in Fredericton. More than 600 Conservatives from across New Brunswick had gathered in the capital city for the meeting. The Student Union Building on the local university campus, where the meeting was taking place, was over-run with Conservatives. In the hallways, the Bricklin collapse was on the lips of many of the delegates. But the mood of the delegates was one of solidarity behind Hatfield. The Conservatives were aware that the Liberal caucus had scheduled a meeting in Fredericton the same afternoon to discuss the Bricklin project, and they were intent on presenting a show of unity. But there was a dissenter.

J.W. Bird, a former Fredericton mayor and reputedly a favored inheritor of a local Conservative nomination whenever Dr. Everett Chalmers, an elderly incumbent, resigned, had been critical of the government's involvement with Bricklin since the project's inception. Bird, who had parlayed a local building supplies and construction business into a regional concern, believed the government should concentrate its efforts on the encouragement of local businesses. He also believed the Bricklin collapse had harmed the Conservative party, and he was prepared to say so. During the business portion of the party's meeting, he got up to urge a resolution of concern about the government's development policies. "What I am about to say may not be popular with many people here today, but it needs saying," Bird began. "It needs saying by someone from within the Conservative party, and it needs saying now, at this meeting, because the credibility of this party and of this province is fast eroding in the wake of the Bricklin failure." Bird paused. "Mr Premier, with the greatest of respect, I must say to you that your description of the Bricklin gamble as merely another respectable effort at economic development is just plain hogwash. It cannot go unchallenged, or every New Brunswicker and every Conservative will be identified with the bad judgment and fiscal irresponsibility to be seen in the Bricklin situation."

By this time, the room was in utter silence. Bird went on. "Lord knows that we do have a seemingly endless source of funds in New Brunswick to promote bankruptcies looking for a place to happen — and the one criterion which apparently applies above all others is that you must be a non-resident to qualify for them. The Bricklin blunder is certainly a characteristic expression of that sad theme . . . " Bird urged the Conservatives, "as a measure of redemption," to approve a motion of concern over the government's development policies, and urge some policy revisions. "Let us be credible as a party and as a province," he said.

There were scattered boos when Bird sat down. "Christ," shouted a Conservative, "he's another Turnbull." Bird's motion died.

Late on the afternoon of September 27, the Opposition Liberals called for the resignation of Hatfield because of "gross mis-management, executive incompetence and deceit" in the Bricklin venture. The Liberals also said they "assumed" that Garvie and Creaghan, the former economic growth minister, would resign "on the grounds of gross misjudgment and mis-management." The Liberals also called for a public inquiry.

Hatfield was approached for a comment on the Liberals' call for his resignation. "Hah, hah," he told a reporter.

In the next week, press reaction set in.

'Bricklin called up yonder,' said a headline in the weekly Woodstock *Bugle,* 'How about Hatfield?'

Claude Bourque, editor of the Moncton French-language daily, *L'Evangeline,* called for a royal commission. "If it had simply been an economic development project," wrote Bourque, "we could forgive Richard Hatfield for much of it, but it was he, and he alone, who chose to risk everything by politicizing the Bricklin. At certain times, it was hard to know who was the real promoter of the project: Malcolm Bricklin or Richard Hatfield." Bourque noted that Hatfield had just left for Japan. "It brings to mind former U.S. president Richard Nixon who in June, 1974, during the worst Watergate crises, flew off to Egypt to be the great diplomat, showing how normal everything was in his country." Bourque concluded that "everything about the Bricklin is beginning to smell of scandal." He called for a royal commission. "It is rather premature to ask for the resignation of Premier Richard Hatfield and his government. Let a royal commission of inquiry decide whether the government acted well or badly."

The Saint John *Telegraph-Journal,* which had fought the Bricklin project bitterly for so many months, escaped into fantasy. On September 27, the day of the Conservative party's annual meeting, the Saint John paper devoted its entire editorial space to Bricklin, under the heading, 'Right, Richard? Right:'

"From the very beginning it had all the touches of a fantasy, a modern day fairy tale with a White Knight riding out of the west, and building his dream castle in New Brunswick — while the people of the province picked up the multi-million dollar tab.

"Others had refused to buy the White Knight's story. They looked on him rather skeptically. Maybe he was too smooth, maybe he was just a silver-tongued promoter. Yes, he was indeed a promoter. He was the first to admit it. In the promotion game, he acknowledged, he excelled.

"He was in fact given the bum's rush in Quebec where he had made his pitch before finding a more friendly and receptive audience in New Brunswick.

"So soon, the White Knight was demonstrating his promotional genius, and the car got unusual exposure all over North America.

"Of course, the picture remained very rosy for anyone wearing rose-tinted glasses, but everyone didn't have tinted glasses and soon the natives were becoming restless. After all, it was their money, and jet-setter Bricklin seemed to be having all the fun. There seemed to be a lot of money going out, and not much, if any, coming in.

"But this was not time to despair. The premier was not about to be influenced by a doomsday thinker. This was a time for confidence in the Bricklin venture, in the government. This was a time for investment and imagination and initiative and enthusiasm — why, this was election time in New Brunswick!

"And there was Premier Richard Hatfield, all smiles, all confidence, as he rode around the province in the symbol of New Brunswick's successful entry into the international automobile manufacturing business. And there he was, smiling out of the television sets with the Bricklin car conveniently in the background. All was well. Had there ever been such a leader?

"But as the premier smiled his smile of confidence and gunned his Bricklin around the province's highways and byways, was everything truly under control? No. Not quite. In fact, Malcolm was back whispering in the premier's ear again and the premier whispered back and the answer was yes and more millions crossed palms and it was agreed that the public need not know about this latest transaction, at least until after the election. They might not understand. Right, Malcolm? Right, Richard. Right.

"But in truth the Bricklin was hurting, almost at death's door as the election date grew nearer and nearer, and politically this was not the time for the Bricklin to cash in its chips. A transfusion of dollars was necessary, and it was made, quietly, without fanfare, without public knowledge. Right, Malcolm? Right, Richard. Right.

"Coldly calculated, politically motivated, the deed was done, and when it became known, after the election, the Liberals were enraged.

"They wanted to know if the premier intended to continue to be conveniently handy and conveniently receptive when Malcolm next whispered in his ear. "What's that, Malcolm, another million? Sure, what are friends for?"

"But now the bubble has burst. The impossible dream has become a nightmare and it is a sad day for New Brunswick, for Bricklin proponents and critics alike, because the province and the people of the province are the real losers.

"Premier Hatfield gambled with our money and he lost. He could have lost in better style if he had not allowed political expediency to cloud his judgment, and all of us would wish that this had been so. If only he had confided in the public more openly and more fully, he would now have more public sympathy. But he chose another road.

"Yesterday the premier was at pains to urge that the people of New Brunswick not let this single setback divert us from the broader picture of industrial development in the province. He just barely drew up short of calling on all of us to get our shoulders to the wheel together."

On October 2, the Clarkson Company, the receiver of Bricklin Canada Ltd., sent a letter to Bricklin's creditors, informing them of their chances of recovering their money. "In the absence of some outside financing, reorganization, or sale of the company, the secured creditors (the province, the Bank of Montreal and the First Pennsylvania Bank) will suffer substantial losses on their claims through a liquidation. Obviously, the ordinary creditors will, in these circumstances, receive nothing."

On October 6, about 200 former employees at Bricklin's Saint John and Minto plants demonstrated on the steps in front of the Centennial Building in Fredericton. The workers had been collecting petitions and they hoped to put pressure on the government to reopen the plants. During a two-hour demonstration, they chanted 'We want our jobs' and presented petitions bearing over 15,000 signatures to Garvie. Garvie said the government was looking for investors to reopen the plants.

Chapter 18

COLLAPSE IN ARIZONA

On Tuesday, October 7, after emerging from his Nebraska weekend-in-residence, Bricklin flew to Toronto where he had scheduled a press conference. Lawyers for General Vehicle Inc. and Bricklin's other U.S. sales companies had filed for time to reorganize the companies under U.S. federal bankruptcy laws. Bricklin had been granted up to thirty days to present a plan to creditors for the continued operation of his companies. If he was not successful — if he could not raise the money to stay in business — the companies would be forced into bankruptcy, and Bricklin, who had provided personal guarantees on his bank and government loans, would have to declare personal bankruptcy. Of course, the U.S. companies depended for their existence on the New Brunswick plants. Bricklin would also have to persuade the New Brunswick government to let him resume business.

The receivership move by New Brunswick had left Bricklin temporarily despondent. "Things look very, very bad," he had admitted to an Associated Press reporter in a September 29 interview. The same day he had told a CBC radio interviewer that he would probably go bankrupt and lose everything. "But what they are not allowed to get are my brains or my drive," he had said glumly. However, the Nebraska weekend, coupled with motivation lectures from Avery, his mentor, had revived Bricklin. When he arrived in Toronto, he was eager to go into business again.

At his Toronto press conference, Bricklin made an offer. He said that "various people who I do business with in the United States on a private basis" were prepared to invest in excess of $10 million in the New Brunswick operations, under certain conditions. The conditions were that the governments of New Brunswick and Canada provide an additional $15 million, and that the New Brunswick government return majority control in Bricklin Canada Ltd. to Bricklin. The governments must also agree not to interfere with Bricklin's operations. The Bricklin companies had been forced to operate "in the political arena" to their detriment, Bricklin said, and his U.S. investors would advance money only if the companies were returned to his control. In response to reporters' questions, Bricklin declined to name his U.S. investors, or even to give their geographic location. He said he had not yet contacted federal or provincial officials with his offer, but that he would do so in the next week.

Bricklin had arranged for several officials of the United Auto Workers Union to attend the press conference, and he praised the New Brunswick workers who had built his cars. For their sakes, he wanted to go into business again. "If it means that I have to roll up my sleeves and go to work on the line with the great people that have built this car," he said, "that will be my pleasure."

Bricklin admitted there was a "good probability" that he would go bankrupt, and that the thought had left him initially in a "severe depression." But, he said, he had checked into the Arizona bankruptcy laws, "and I found that I get to keep five milk cows and two dray horses, and I started getting very optimistic and people talked to me and said, 'What, are you nuts, I mean you are going to be in bankruptcy.' And I said yes, except that I remember and I get to see the car. I remember the great people that put it together. You are seeing for the first time how it really can work . . . How the UAW and management started the car together and are now together fighting to keep that car alive. And that car will stay alive."

Jack Taylor, a senior UAW official who had taken part in negotiations for the first collective agreement signed with Bricklin, was with Bricklin at the press conference. He made a plea that the New Brunswick government reconsider its position and invest more money in the Bricklin plants. "The kind of a union that we are," said Taylor, "a bread and butter gut union, the auto workers union, a union good to our worth, I think a good faith union and a good clean union, we are going to do everything possible within our power and whatever way we can to make sure that that automobile is a success by being manufactured and assembled, produced and retooled in Canada. And I plead, I plead with the political people today to give the opportunity to Mr. Bricklin. Give the opportunity to the 700 workers in Saint John (there were 500), who, for two years this coming December, have made a great input to that particular product. Yes, the political people, and I don't want to play games here, but the political people have had some fun over this particular automobile, and it is not fun when it comes to a pay cheque every Friday."

After the press conference, Bricklin attempted to contact the New Brunswick government with his offer. He was told that people such as Garvie were in meetings and couldn't talk to him. Hatfield was still in Japan. Garvie did send a telegram to Bricklin in connection with Bricklin's claim that he had found investors in the U.S. "Identify the sources of the ten million dollars in financing available in the U.S. and have these principals contact the department directly, and provide the department with a satisfactory operating plan as requested in August."

Bricklin's credibility gap was too wide for even the New Brunswick government, the last of the believers.

Three weeks later, with his U.S. network of companies drifting towards bankruptcy and with no money available to rescue them, Bricklin prepared to meet his U.S. creditors. On October 31, in the Phoenix law offices of Treon, Warnicke and Mann, he signed a deposition accompanying declarations and financial statements that would be submitted to the U.S. District Court in Phoenix, Arizona, in connection with a creditors' hearing. The deposition said, in effect, that Bricklin didn't have intimate knowledge of the financial affairs of his companies. The financial statements filed with the court were incomplete. Many of the accounting records of General Vehicle Inc. and its subsidiary companies were still spread across the United States. They were coming to Phoenix in boxloads from such places as Whippany and Livonia, and Leon Klein was sorting them.

On November 10, creditors of Bricklin's U.S. companies held their first meeting before Judge Edward E. Davis of the U.S. District Court, bankruptcy division, in Phoenix. Bricklin attended. He had not been able to prepare a reorganization plan for his companies and would ask for more time. Robert Jarrett, who had been appointed receiver of the companies, reported that he was selling Bricklin parts because of a "great demand" from dealers for them. Bricklin took the stand before Judge Davis and recounted circumstances that he said had led to the collapse of Bricklin Canada Ltd. He said that, with the First Pennsylvania Bank and the province unable to decide who would loan $10 million to him, Garvie "took it upon himself" to instruct Ralph Henry not to ship cars from New Brunswick. "He (Garvie) informed me that he informed Ralph Henry, our president, that the Royal Canadian Mounted Police would be called to put Mr. Henry in jail if, in fact, he did move any cars," Bricklin told the court. "With that, I could not recommend that our president take this particular gamble."

Bricklin said he believed his U.S. companies could launch claims for more than $25 million against New Brunswick because of the receivership decision. However, he hadn't decided if he would press the claims.

After Bricklin's testimony, the creditors' hearing adjourned. Judge Davis granted Bricklin until December 15 to present a reorganization plan. The creditors would meet again on that date.

On November 17, the First Pennsylvania Bank, the major secured creditor of Bricklin's U.S. companies, began a court action to take control of the Bricklin assets in the U.S. The move would result in bankruptcy for Bricklin and his Delaware companies. The bank would take everything.

On November 18, 1975, exactly a year after the Conservative government was returned to power in a Bricklin car, the New Brunswick legislature began a fall sitting. The government had adjourned the spring session of the legislature until November in anticipation of federal initiatives in the fall — possibly an interim budget — to cool off the economy. In October, Prime Minister Trudeau had announced a system of wage and price controls to slow inflation. The New Brunswick government quickly threw its support behind the controls and made preparations to use the fall sitting of the legislature to publicise them. But the government would be unable to avoid debate on one of its own inflationary actions — a $23 million investment in Bricklin that would saddle New Brunswick's taxpayers with additional debts and interest payments for years.

In the seven weeks since Bricklin Canada Ltd. was placed in receivership, government spokesmen had hinted frequently that new investors would open the Bricklin plants. Like Bricklin, the government spokesmen had declined to name their potential investors. Hatfield had said in October that several Canadian investors' groups were showing an "intense and serious interest" in the Bricklin project. New Brunswick officials were meeting with the groups in Toronto on a daily basis. In November, Garvie had said that negotiations to resurrect the project had expanded to include additional groups of investors, some with foreign involvement. But he declined to name them. But while the government was pursuing its negotiations, the First Pennsylvania Bank was taking steps to unload the Bricklin assets at Saint John and Minto. On November 14, four days before the fall sitting began, the bank closed tenders on the sale of assets, which included all the cars, parts and materials at the two plants. The New Brunswick government was left with the body moulds. Any new investor would have to start from scratch.

On November 18, shortly after prayers, Garvie rose in the legislature to report on the Bricklin project. He said the government was continuing its negotiations with potential investors in Toronto and with "certain overseas companies" to revive the project. He didn't name any of the companies. He said the government was in possession of studies that showed the Bricklin plants could be operated viably on a production schedule of 5,000 cars per year, in contrast to the 30,000 that Bricklin had dreamed of building each year. Garvie said that limited production, with an emphasis on car quality, would ensure that the New Brunswick-built car would remain unique and marketable "for many years to come." He noted that The First Pennsylvania Bank had closed tenders on the sale of assets from the New Brunswick plants, but said this didn't present an insurmountable problem. It might even be an advantage, he ventured, because potential investors who were holding back would realize the government wasn't going to panic. Garvie said that Aston Martin Ltd., an English car company, had been shut down recently for six months before new capital revived it. "We are prepared to wait an equal or longer period to achieve the same positive results," he said. In the meantime, the government didn't intend to endanger the "delicate" negotiations to revive Bricklin by making imprudent disclosures. In other words, the government wouldn't make public the documents and financial statements that it knew the Liberals were seeking.

After Garvie's statement, the Liberals presented notices of motion seeking Bricklin documents. The Liberal motions would come up for debate on December 9. The debate would drag on for three days, concluding on December 12, the day that Malcolm Bricklin would file for personal bankruptcy in an Arizona court. By then, the First Pennsylvania Bank would have sold Bricklin's New Brunswick assets to a Columbus, Ohio company that specialized in the block purchase of distressed lots of vehicles. The company, Consolidated International Ltd., intended to sell the Bricklins and supply parts.

Before the government voted down the Liberal motions, Turnbull stood up to announce that he had found "the hooker" in the Bricklin project. He said that, watching Bricklin, he had often felt like a city slicker at a country fair, watching a shell game. "How is Malcolm gettin' the money? How is Malcolm gettin' the money?" Turnbull paused. "My God," he said, "You don't know where the pea is!" Turnbull said he had finally found the shell with the pea under it. "The answer is so simple — he bought the cars and he didn't pay for them." Turnbull estimated that at least $5 million had not been returned to New Brunswick for car shipments. Turnbull laughed aloud.

Chapter 19

BRICKLIN'S BANKRUPTCY

On December 12, while members of the New Brunswick legislature were kicking his name around, Malcolm Bricklin filed personal bankruptcy papers in a Phoenix court. Bricklin had no choice. The First Pennsylvania Bank had seized and sold the inventory of Bricklin Canada Ltd. The New Brunswick government had locked him out. The bank had laid claim to Bricklin's U.S. assets. Bricklin was left with nothing.

In his bankruptcy statement, Bricklin described himself as an unemployed automobile executive. His residence was no longer the exclusive Scottsdale Hilton home that he had rented shortly after he received his first New Brunswick financing in 1973. His new address was 3800 East Lincoln Drive, Apt. 15. In a section of his statement dealing with transfers of property, Bricklin stated that he had reached a property settlement with his wife, Brenda, in the past month. Bricklin was divorcing his wife. Under the same section, Bricklin noted that "Colleen McCabe, the bankrupt's girlfriend, has received occasional presents in the past two years that they have been dating."

Bricklin's bankruptcy petition listed personal debts of $32.3 million and assets of $2,000. Among secured creditors, Bricklin listed debts of $23 million "approximately" owing to Provincial Holdings Ltd., the New Brunswick agency that had provided funds to Bricklin Canada Ltd. Bricklin had given personal guarantees on the loans from the province. He listed a debt of $6 million owing to the First Pennsylvania Bank, $21,000 to the Lincoln National Bank of Philadelphia, and $75,000 to David Zeitlin of Pennsauken, New Jersey, who had made a personal loan to Bricklin secured by Subaru shares.

Bricklin's list of debts to unsecured creditors was two pages long and totaled $3.3 million. It reads like a road map to the high life. He owed $2,390 to Diner's Club, $1,000 to Carte Blanche and $1,000 to BankAmericard. He owed $1,900 to the Indian Trials Horse Country Club and $1,786 to Atlantic Pacific Leasing. His largest unsecured debt was to Leon Stern for $2.75 million, in connection with Stern's 1974 breach-of-contract suit against Bricklin. Bricklin owed another debt of $206,931 to Rusar, Inc., a company belonging to the New York Koffman family which had forced him out of Subaru.

In a schedule of personal property, Bricklin listed his assets of $2,000. These included a rifle, clothes, a watch, skis and "miscellaneous personal effects."

On a separate page, Bricklin listed another asset. "The bankrupt has licensed his name in the past but said licence has been cancelled," he said. "He claims the right to use his name as a personal attribute not subject to the use or sale by the bankruptcy Trustee." Bricklin didn't want his name to be used on cars built by anyone else.

On December 15, three days after he filed his bankruptcy petition, Bricklin issued a press release in which he announced that he was resigning from his positions with Bricklin Canada Ltd., General Vehicle Inc. and his other U.S. sales companies. "I regret that I can be of no further service to General Vehicle Inc., its subsidiaries and the Province of New Brunswick," said his press release, which was given to reporters by his sister, Barbara Jonas. "I am resigning because the First Pennsylvania Bank petitioned the court not to spend additional monies on the future development of General Vehicle Inc. and the Bricklin SV-1."

Bricklin said in his statement that he was on the verge of a new career. He was going to develop a revolutionary new car engine. "Although I have lost all my personal financial resources," he said, "I plan to remain working toward the betterment of transportation through the development of a revolutionary new engine." Bricklin had connected with Frank Turner, a Graham, Texas engineer who had invented a new type of rotary engine that would weigh less, use less gas and emit less pollution than conventional engines. The engine would be called the Bricklin-Turner power plant, and Bricklin would begin to look for money to manufacture it.

On the day of Bricklin's announcement, creditors of General Vehicle Inc. held their second hearing in the Phoenix court of Judge Davis. Ron Warnicke, the lawyer for GVI and its associated companies, informed the creditors that Bricklin had resigned from the companies because of the moves by the First Pennsylvania Bank to take security. Warnicke ventured that it might be in "everyone's interest" to put General Vehicle and its subsidiaries into bankruptcy. "Mr. Bricklin will co-operate within the means available to him," Warnicke said, "However, the bulk of his efforts, naturally, in order to earn a living, are going to have to be directed in other ways."

Philip Berelson, a lawyer for the First Pennsylvania Bank, informed the creditors that the bank was laying claims to the assets of GVI "and if, as is expected, the bank's claim does extend to virtually all of those assets, it would appear that there is no hope, whatsoever, of having to reorganize. I just want to point that out, today." The bank was taking everything.

The creditors' hearing then adjourned until January 12, 1976, at which time it would be decided whether to plunge General Vehicle and its subsidiaries into bankruptcy.

On December 17, the last day of the 1976 session of the New Brunswick legislature, the Liberals read press reports of Bricklin's bankruptcy and his new plans. Joseph Daigle, the Liberals' financial critic, posed a question in the House to Stewart Brooks, the treasury board minister. "Would you advise if you have under consideration applications for investment in a new industry to develop a revolutionary engine in New Brunswick?"

"Not that I know of," Brooks said.

"Don't answer the phone," Turnbull shouted.

"No, it might be Malcolm," Graham said.

Chapter 20

Cost of Gull-Wings

Bricklin Canada Ltd. remains in receivership. Nearly two years after Bricklin's collapse, the New Brunswick government maintains the position that efforts to revive the company would be harmed if the government released the Bricklin accounting records or its own Bricklin files. To prevent legal entanglements, the government has purchased the remaining shares in Bricklin Canada Ltd., at an undisclosed price, to become its sole owner. The government has also written a $51,000 cheque for vacation pay owed to Bricklin's plant workers. The cheque was required to protect Bricklin Canada Ltd. from bankruptcy — a New Brunswick court had ordered the company to pay the workers. In recent months, government officials have asserted that they remain optimistic about the prospects for reviving a car industry in New Brunswick. They are the last of the optimists. Bricklin's dreams have become albatrosses for many people, and Bricklin's car is now the government's albatross.

The losses are still being counted. Bricklin's U.S. companies listed debts of $34.6 million when they were finally declared bankrupt in Phoenix on January 12, 1976. The companies listed tangible assets of $1.6 million. The list of General Vehicle Inc. creditors was more than 50 pages long. About $26-million was owed to the province of New Brunswick and the First Pennsylvania Bank, by virtue of guarantees provided by the U.S. companies on loans to Bricklin Canada Ltd. Bricklin car dealers were owed $1.5-million for parts and advertising that Bricklin didn't deliver. Dealers and car buyers were owed an estimated $3 million for warranty claims on Bricklin cars. Various suppliers were owed $929,000, and U.S. employees of Bricklin were owed $133,000 in unpaid wages.

The losses suffered by Bricklin Canada Ltd. are not known because the government has declined to release the company's accounting records. The province's loss is estimated at $23-million, which is the amount of public financing provided to the company. The losses suffered by individual creditors of Bricklin Canada Ltd. are not known, but an estimate can be made. According to figures in the 1975 budget prepared by Clarkson Gordon for the Bricklin companies, Bricklin Canada Ltd. owed its suppliers at least $4.6 million on June 30, 1975. According to Bricklin company sources, the debts to suppliers rose to at least $6 million by September, when Bricklin was placed in receivership. According to the sources, few bills were paid by the New

Brunswick company in the summer of 1975. Large numbers of bills simply piled up on desks or were thrown into boxes in the weeks before receivership, according to the sources. The bills were still arriving after the company was shut down.

Some of the consequences of Bricklin's collapse are becoming apparent. For a province of 670,000 people, they are enormous. New Brunswick's entire development program has been placed under a strain. The province will have to borrow on American markets to repay its $23 million investment in Bricklin Canada Ltd. It is a burden that the province's taxpayers will carry with difficulty. Already, the effects of the losses on New Brunswick's treasury are discernible. The government, because of its losses on Bricklin and on a number of smaller investments in the past two years, has been forced to reduce its investment activity. According to government and industry sources, loan applications from companies are being turned down with increasing regularity. The government hasn't got the money. According to bank sources, the province's credibility has suffered in financial circles. Banks are not as willing to provide guaranteed loans because they have less faith in the government's business judgments.

Beyond references to world conditions and start-up problems, the government has offered few explanations for Bricklin's collapse. But some of the factors are obvious. They were inherent in the project. One is the simple problem of distances. Parts and materials for Bricklin cars were imported to New Brunswick from sources as distant as California. Cars were assembled at two New Brunswick plants for shipment to distant markets. An efficient organization would have been required to overcome the high overhead costs imposed by geography. The Bricklin organization was not efficient. It was as disparate and as unco-ordinated as the Bricklin parts supply. The Bricklin car was designed in Livonia, Michigan, because Bricklin had rented a plant there before he came to New Brunswick. Cars were assembled at Saint John and Minto because Bricklin received financing from New Brunswick to assemble them there. Financial records were maintained in New York because Joe Rose, Bricklin's chief financial adviser, had his offices there. The entire operation was directed, after a fashion, from Phoenix, Arizona, because Bricklin, the Philadelphia kid, had decided to move west and become a cowboy.

Another factor in the collapse was the project's management. It was inadequate, if not incompetent. Bricklin didn't understand the problems involved in the engineering of a car. He attempted to go into production without a completed production model. Albert Bricklin was no help. New Brunswick officials didn't know the difference. They thought Bricklin was ready to produce the car they saw in his short film.

They accepted a value of $1 million for Bricklin's design and manufacturing rights, and then proceeded to pay most of the costs of designing a manufacturing model of his car. The people who had some knowledge of the production problems weren't given authority to handle them. People like Jean de Villers and Jack Hennessey were overruled constantly by the Bricklins. The government had the authority to correct the management problems, but it took the position initially that it wasn't in the car business, although it was prepared to finance one. By late 1974, when the government reversed its position and attempted to exercise control over the project, it was too late. The Bricklin hierarchy and structure of operations was too firmly established. As late as August, 1975, the government would attempt to impose management controls on Bricklin, without success.

Other factors are contained possibly in the accounting records of Bricklin Canada Ltd., which the government refuses to release, and in government documents, which the government refuses to release. The accounting records would indicate the amount of money diverted from production in New Brunswick to support Bricklin's U.S. companies. They would record, in some fashion, the inter-company transfers of funds between New Brunswick and the U.S. They would indicate the frills and bloated salaries which are suggested in the 1975 Clarkson Gordon budget for the Bricklin companies. The government files would disclose the projections and the information upon which the government advanced money to Bricklin. They would disclose government perceptions of problems in the Bricklin operations, particularly in 1975 when the government was receiving weekly reports from its consultants on the project. The government refuses to make these records and documents public.

Bricklin, the man who left so many debts, is still riding the range. He is promoting a new rotary engine, invented by Frank Turner, a Graham, Texas, engineer. Bricklin is intrigued by the engine. It contains 12 cylinders and "works something like the principles of a six-gun," he said in a recent speech to promote the engine. He has bought world rights from Turner for the engine. He calls it the Bricklin Rotary Vee. He is looking for investors.

The political consequences of the Bricklin collapse are uncertain. It is unlikely that Hatfield will drive a Bricklin car in the next New Brunswick election. However, he may be carrying one on his back.

A Note On Sources

Much of the information in this book is based on interviews with sources within the Bricklin organization. Those sources have to be protected. Other information was obtained in interviews with government officials, in government documents, in court records, and in the thousands of pages of newspaper and magazine coverage of Malcolm Bricklin and his car. Among the magazine articles, two are worth special mention. One is an article by Barry Rosenberg, entitled 'Would You Buy A Used Car From This Man?', which appeared in the April, 1975 issue of *Philadelphia Magazine,* providing the first substantial account of Bricklin's life in business. The second is an article by Steve Spence, entitled 'Adventures Along the Yellow Bricklin Road', which appeared in the November, 1975 issue of *Motor Trend.*

Special acknowledgement is made to Mercey Brothers Publishing for permission to quote from the record, *'The Bricklin and Other Sound Investments',* by Charlie Russell.

SOURCES

(1) Government Documents

Provincial Holdings Ltd. — Bricklin financial agreements; *Royal Gazette,* Province of New Brunswick; Orders-in-council, Province of New Brunswick; *Synoptic Reports* of the Legislative Assembly, Province of New Brunswick; Reports of Public Accounts Committees, New Brunswick Legislative Assembly; Memoranda and Reports, New Brunswick Multiplex Corp.; Reports, New Brunswick Research and Productivity Council; New Brunswick Information Service.

(2) Magazines

Philadelphia Magazine; Gallery; Popular Mechanics; Coronet; Saga; Playboy; Car and Driver; Motor Trend; Advertising Age; Macleans; Canadian Machinery and Metalworking; Road and Track; People; Road Test; Automotive News.

(3) Newspapers

The Telegraph-Journal and *Evening Times-Globe,* Saint John; *The Daily Gleaner,* Fredericton; *The Times and The Transcript,* Moncton; *L'Evangeline,* Moncton; *Financial Times of Canada; The Financial Post;* Montreal *Star; The Globe and Mail,* Toronto; Toronto *Star; Le Devoir,* Montreal; Boston *Sunday Globe;* Hartland *Observer; Kings County Record;* Woodstock *Bugle; The Northern Light,* Bathurst.

(4) Court Records

California Superior Court; U.S. District Court in Orlando, Florida; U.S. District Court in New Jersey; U.S. District Court in Philadelphia, Pennsylvania; U.S. District Court in Phoenix, Arizona; New Brunswick Supreme Court.